About the Author

Bill Thompson is Vice-President of Scott Advertising & Publishing Co., and editor of CERAMIC Arts & Crafts and CERAMIC Teaching Projects & Trade News magazines, as well as author of THE FUNDAMENTALS OF HOBBY CERAMICS, a hardbound book released by this publisher in 1975.

Mr. Thompson has been teaching, writing and exhibiting his work in china painting and ceramics for many, many years, and has garnered an impressive number of honors and awards. We are proud to have him as a member of our hard-working staff.

Lois Scott
Scott Advertising & Publishing Co.
Livonia, Michigan

THE BASICS OF CHINA PAINTING

by Bill Thompson

Material published in this book is reprinted from
CERAMIC Arts & Crafts magazine, a monthly publication
serving the ceramic and china painting industries. All
rights reserved. No part of this book may be reproduced
in any form or by any means, electronic or mechanical,
including photocopying, recording, or by any information
storage and retrieval system, without permission in
writing from the publisher.

Inquiries should be addressed to
Scott Advertising & Publishing Co.
30595 West 8 Mile Road
Livonia, Michigan 48152

Copyright © 1976 by Scott Advertising & Publishing Co.
30595 W. 8 Mile Road, Livonia, Michigan 48152

Printed in the United States of America

THE BASICS OF CHINA PAINTING

by Bill Thompson

CONTENTS

COLOR PLATES

PLATE 1
SEE PAGE 47

7

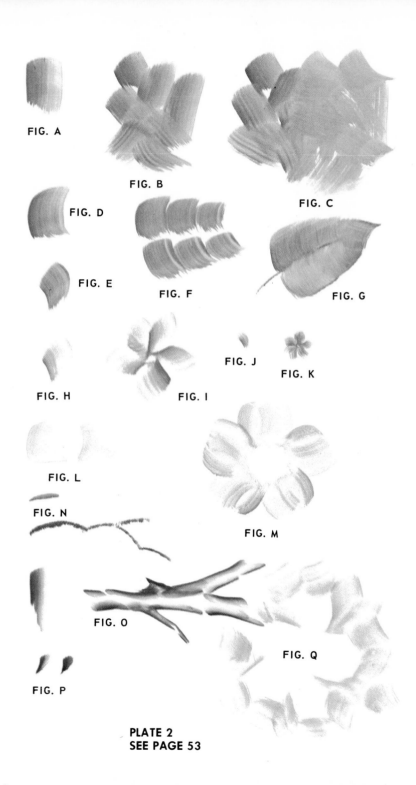

FIG. A

FIG. B

FIG. C

FIG. D

FIG. E

FIG. F

FIG. G

FIG. H

FIG. I

FIG. J

FIG. K

FIG. L

FIG. N

FIG. M

FIG. O

FIG. Q

FIG. P

PLATE 2
SEE PAGE 53

PLATE 3
SEE PAGE 61

PLATE 4
SEE PAGE 69

PLATE 5
SEE PAGE 75

11

	YELLOW GREEN	OLIVE GREEN	BROWN GREEN	BLACK GREEN	SHADING GREEN	DEEP BLUE GREEN	MIXING YELLOW	YELLOW BROWN LIGHT	YELLOW BROWN DARK	RICH BROWN	DARK BROWN	PINK	DARK PINK	RUBY	YELLOW RED	BLOOD RED	POMPADOUR	VIOLET OR IRON	PALE VIOLET	DARK VIOLET	MAUVE	PALE BLUE	DARK BLUE	BLACK
YELLOW GREEN																								
OLIVE GREEN																								
BROWN GREEN																								
BLACK GREEN																								
SHADING GREEN																								
DEEP BLUE GREEN																								
MIXING YELLOW																								
YELLOW BROWN LIGHT																								
YELLOW BROWN DARK																								
RICH BROWN																								
DARK BROWN																								
PINK																								
DARK PINK																								
RUBY																								
YELLOW RED																								
BLOOD RED																								
POMPADOUR																								
VIOLET OF IRON																								
PALE VIOLET																								
DARK VIOLET																								
MAUVE																								
PALE BLUE																								
DARK BLUE																								
BLACK																								

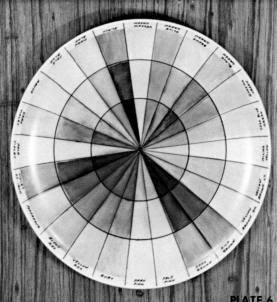

**PLATE 6
SEE PAGE 81**

PLATE 7
SEE PAGE 87

13

PLATE 8
SEE PAGE 101

14

PLATE 9
SEE PAGE 101

15

PLATE 10
SEE PAGE 107

16

PLATE 11
SEE PAGE 123

17

PLATE 12
SEE PAGE 129

18

PLATE 13
SEE PAGE 135

19

PLATE 14
SEE PAGE 141

21

PLATE 15
SEE PAGE 151

PLATE 16
SEE PAGE 151

23

PLATE 17
SEE PAGE 159

PLATE 18
SEE PAGE 159

25

PLATE 19
SEE PAGE 163

26

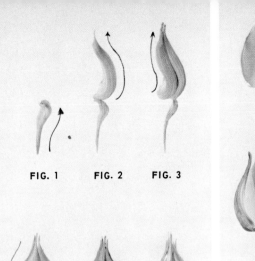

FIG. 1   FIG. 2   FIG. 3

FIG. 4   FIG. 5 __   FIG. 6

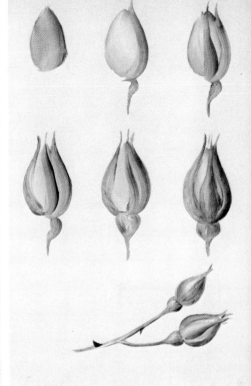

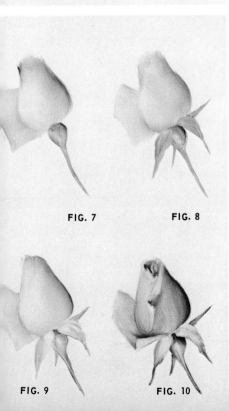

FIG. 7   FIG. 8

FIG. 9   FIG. 10

PLATE 20
SEE PAGE 163

PLATE 21
SEE PAGE 167

28

PLATE 22
SEE PAGE 167

29

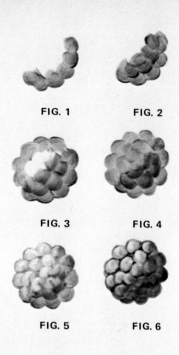

FIG. 1   FIG. 2

FIG. 3   FIG. 4

FIG. 5   FIG. 6

PLATE 23
SEE PAGE 175

PLATE 24
SEE PAGE 175

PLATE 25
SEE PAGE 181

PLATE 26
SEE PAGE 181

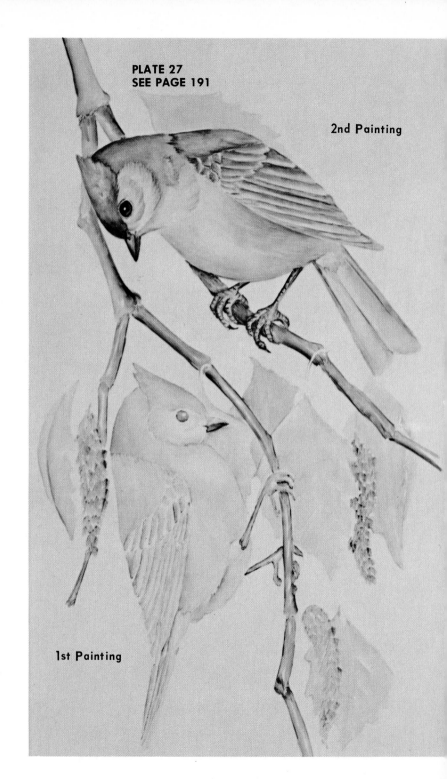

PLATE 27
SEE PAGE 191

2nd Painting

1st Painting

PLATE 28
SEE PAGE 191

PLATE 29
SEE PAGE 197

2nd Painting

1st Painting

PLATE 30
SEE PAGE 197

Bill Thompson

PLATE 31
SEE PAGE 203

2nd Painting

1st Painting

PLATE 32
SEE PAGE 203

PLATE 33
SEE PAGE 211

2nd Painting

1st Painting

PLATE 34
SEE PAGE 211

41

PLATE 35
SEE PAGE 217

PLATE 36
SEE PAGE 217

PLATE 37
SEE PAGE 223

44

PLATE 38
SEE PAGE 229

45

Introduction

SEE COLOR PLATE 1, PAGE 7

China painting — the decoration of porcelain and ceramic ware with overglaze colors — is an ancient art, but a relative newcomer to the crafts field. Overglaze colors in the form of enamels were used in the latter part of the Sung Dynasty (A.D. 960-1279), to embellish the pottery of that period; the first pieces so decorated were the porcelains of Tz'u Chow in the province of Honan. The colors used were limited to primitive reds, greens and yellows. These same colors were also used at the same time in Persia, and it has never been decided whether the Chinese or Persians were the first ones to use these materials.

When European potters finally learned to make porcelain, overglaze colors were employed as the decorating media for much of their wares; the output of pieces decorated in this manner reached its peak during the 1700's in Italy, France, Germany and the Netherlands.

The most commonly used term for overglaze colors today is "china paints," since they are almost always applied to white porcelain "china," but these materials have been known by a variety of other names, such as mineral colors, colors of the "petit feu" (low temperature), enamel colors and muffle colors (the latter name coming from the type of kiln — a muffle kiln — in which they were fired).

It was not until 1873 that china painting began as a craft in this country, when Karl Langenbeck, of Cincinnati, Ohio, received some china-painting colors from his uncle, in Germany. Maria Longworth Nichols, who was later to found the famous Rookwood Pottery, was a neighbor of Karl's, and was intrigued with this new art to the point where she imported some of the colors for herself and her friends.

In 1874, Mr. Ben Pitman, an instructor at the Cincinnati School of Design, obtained a supply of china paints and other necessary materials, and engaged a Miss Eggers to teach china painting to a group of young women; Miss Eggers had become familiar with overglaze decoration while in Dresden, Germany. Enthusiastically received, the new craft became a most popular pastime, and culminated in the first exhibit of hand-painted china on May 25, 1875, in Cincinnati. Miss Louise McLaughlin, one of the original group of china painters, published the first book on the subject, calling it "China Painting – a Practical Manual for the Use of Amateurs in the Decoration of Hard Porcelain." Before long, classes were in progress throughout the eastern part of this country, and soon the names Stewart, Aulich, Safford, Leykauf, Fry, Filkins, Robineau and others became recognized as masters of the art. China painting has continued in popularity, and is today practiced by people in all walks of life.

China paints are composed of color pigments mixed with a glaze medium, and a flux to lower the melting point of the colors below that of the glaze to which they are applied.

When the colors are subjected to heat in the 1330° to 1530°F range (cone 018-014), the flux causes them to melt and fuse with the fired-on glaze of the decorated item. Most china paints do not change color when fired, but do, when properly fired, acquire a gloss.

Compounded as finely ground powders, china paints must be mixed, or ground with a medium to render them suitable to brush application. Any one of a number of oils can be used to grind the dry colors, the most popular being a mixture composed of copaiba and other oils, usually oils of lavender and clove. Copaiba is an oleoresin obtained from several species of South American trees, and is a transparent liquid that can vary in color from pale yellow to golden, and has an aromatic fragrance; this oil is known as copaiba balsam, or balsam of copaiba, indicating that it flows from the trees in a spontaneous manner and is not a distillate.

Many commercially prepared oils for mixing and applying china paints are available, and are compounded to be fast or slow-drying, thick or thin, and for specific techniques. Most painters, after some experimentation, choose one oil medium that best suits their style of painting, while others prefer to compound oils to fit their particular needs. It has been said that there are as many oils as there are painters; though this is an exaggeration, you will find painters using salad oil, olive oil, mineral oil, lubricating oil — anything and everything imaginable, in an attempt to discover the "magic" ingredient to make them proficient painters. Beginning china painters will be well advised to use the materials recommended in this series until the techniques described have been mastered.

BASIC SUPPLIES

The materials needed for china painting are readily available, and the following list of supplies is recommended as a basic outfit. Beginners who progress will no doubt wish to acquire additional colors and brushes.

Palette — A palette for china painting is usually a metal box (with a cover), fitted with a piece of opal glass or clear glass over white paper, on which small mounds of the mixed paints are placed.

Palette Knife — A small palette knife, with a flexible blade about 2-1/2" long, used to grind and/or mix the powdered colors with the medium.

Ground Glass Slab — A piece of glass which is smooth on one side and dull, or "ground," on the other. Most powdered colors can be mixed with the medium on the smooth side of the glass; colors that tend to be grainy, such as ruby and purples, are ground smooth on the textured side.

Overglaze colors — Packaged in vials, the powdered paints are available in literally hundreds of colors. Beginners should become familiar with the colors listed here, and later may wish to try some of the others to develop a palette to suit a personal style of painting. Ready-mixed colors are available, for those who prefer to eliminate the need for grinding and mixing them.

Yellow green.
Olive green.
Brown green.
Black green.
Shading green.
Deep blue green.
Mixing yellow.
Yellow brown light.
Yellow brown deep.
Rich brown.

Dark brown.
Pink.
Dark pink.
Ruby.
Yellow red.
Blood red.
Pompadour.
Violet of iron.
Pale violet.
Dark violet.
Mauve.
Pale blue.
Dark blue.
Black.

Medium – An all-purpose oil medium, to be used for mixing the powdered overglaze colors as well as for painting.

Brushes – Square shader quill brushes, sizes #4, #6 and #10; a #2 liner and a #00 red sable.

The hairs of quill brushes are fastened into the quills of turkey, chicken and goose feathers, and are supplied with separate wooden handles. The quill portions of the brushs, NOT the bristles, should be soaked in hot water, to soften them before inserting the handles. It may also be necessary to sand or scrape the handles to fit the quills.

Turpentine – Pour an inch or two of artist's quality, pure gum turpentine into a small jar, for washing brushes and palette knife. The turpentine in the jar will remain usable for a long time, but tends to acquire an oily feel after continued use; the cost of turpentine is minimal, so the jar can and should be kept filled with fresh, clean turpentine.

Denatured Alcohol – China should be wiped with a cloth dampened with alcohol before being painted, to be sure that it is clean and free from oil and grease. Brushes used with gold should also be cleaned in a (separate) jar of alcohol.

Lint-Free Cloth – A pad of lint-free cloth is used to remove excess oil and paint from brushes. Old linen napkins and tablecloths from resale shops make excellent paint cloths, as do old, much-washed huck towels and cotton sheets.

China Silk – Fine-textured, pure silk is used for patting background colors, and for wiping highlights from painted china. Several pieces of silk about 9" square should be included in a china painting kit, and can be washed and reused until the material wears out.

Fine Sandpaper – China should be sanded with fine

sandpaper each time it has been fired, to remove any surface roughness.

Absorbent Cotton – Absorbent cotton covered by a piece of china silk is used to pat freshly applied paint when "tinting" backgrounds for china painting. Store the cotton in a plastic bag, so that none of the fibers will get into the paint or onto the painting cloths.

China Marking Pencil – A pencil which can be used to sketch a design onto the china; be sure to purchase this pencil from a china painting supplier, since the marks of some pencils sold at office supplies stores will not disappear when the china is fired.

Tracing Paper – Semi-transparent paper on which to trace designs which can later be transferred to china.

Graphite Paper – Used to transfer designs to china (DO NOT use carbon paper).

Liquid Bright Gold – This gold is a lustre which fires to a bright, brassy finish, and is used primarily as a base for Roman Gold.

Roman (burnish) Gold – Sold in small boxes containing a glass slab on which is a dark brown paste; this paste is real gold and fires to a dull yellow, frosted appearance, which must be polished to obtain the characteristic coin gold look. (NOTE: Although not too commonly used, Roman Gold is available in liquid form.)

Brushes for Gold – Separate brushes must be used for applying gold, and should be labeled and stored with the gold supplies. A small square shader brush and a liner brush will be sufficient for most gold work.

Gold Facilitator – Medium for Roman Gold.

FIRING

When the colors have been mixed and applied to the china, the piece must be fired in a kiln, so that the colors mature and fuse with the glaze of the decorated piece. Until the end of World War II, most china painters fired their wares, or had them fired by local potteries, in kilns that used gas or kerosene for fuel. The advent of the inexpensive, lightweight electric kiln, in the late 1940's, made it possible for almost any china painter to have and fire his or her own kiln.

Procedures

SEE COLOR PLATE 2, PAGE 8

John Wesley, the English clergyman and founder of Methodism, said in one of his sermons: "Cleanliness is, indeed, next to godliness." Cleanliness in china painting is important if the painter wishes to produce attractive, unblemished work. The oils used to mix and apply china paints tend to attract dust and lint, which, if allowed to settle on freshly painted ware, cause specks and spots that cannot be covered or removed once the china has been fired. The obvious prevention of this problem is to have the work area and materials as clean as possible. The palette, oil jar and turpentine should be covered when not in use, brushes should be cleaned at the end of each painting session, and the work area should be clean and uncluttered.

PREPARING THE PALETTE: As stated in the previous chapter, the most commonly used type of palette is a flat, metal box with a cover, fitted with a glass slab to hold the mixed paints; an acceptable substitute is a piece of glass cut to fit into a flat cardboard box which has a cover, or into a cookie pan with a second cookie pan to serve as a cover.

To save time while painting, the colors should always be placed in the same positions on the palette, each time the palette is cleaned or fresh colors are mixed. Until the painter learns to recognize each color at a glance, the color names can be written on the glass with the china marking pencil (see Photo 1). For palettes furnished with clear glass, the color names can be written on a sheet of

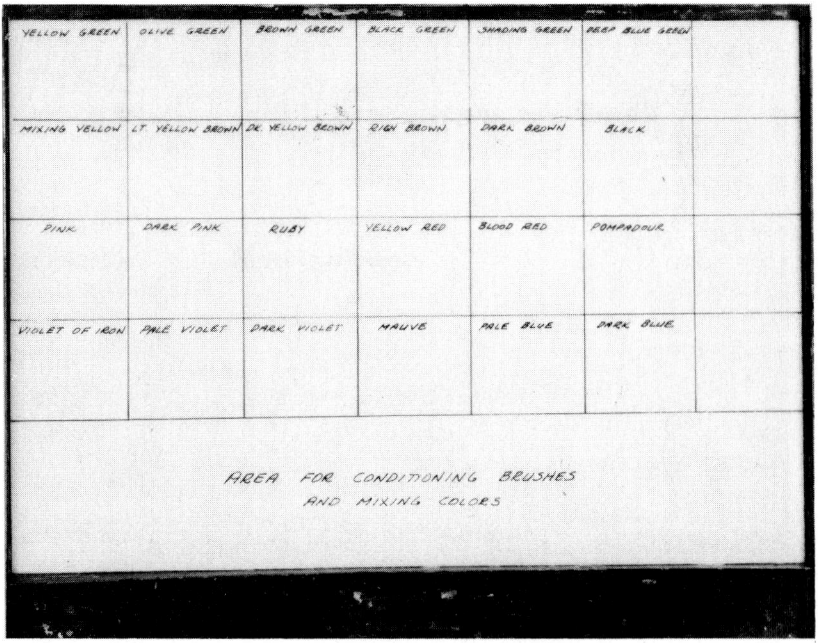

YELLOW GREEN	OLIVE GREEN	BROWN GREEN	BLACK GREEN	SHADING GREEN	DEEP BLUE GREEN
MIXING YELLOW	LT. YELLOW BROWN	DK YELLOW BROWN	RICH BROWN	DARK BROWN	BLACK
PINK	DARK PINK	RUBY	YELLOW RED	BLOOD RED	POMPADOUR
VIOLET OF IRON	PALE VIOLET	DARK VIOLET	MAUVE	PALE BLUE	DARK BLUE

AREA FOR CONDITIONING BRUSHES AND MIXING COLORS

PHOTO 1

Palette marked with color names.

plain white paper, to be placed under the glass.

MIXING THE PAINTS: If powdered china paints are used, they must be mixed with oil to the correct consistency for painting (mixed paints should have the consistency of toothpaste). A small amount of powdered paint is placed on the ground glass slab, and a few drops of oil are added to it. The color and oil are thoroughly mixed with the palette knife, using the flat of the knife blade to mix the color with a circular motion (see Photo 2). It is important that the oil be added just a few drops at a time, so that the mixed color does not become thin and runny; if too much oil is inadvertently used, enough powdered paint should be added to the mixture to bring it to the proper consistency.

The mixed paint is scooped up with the edge of the palette knife, and placed in its position on the palette. Pressure is applied to the knife as it is drawn forward, depositing the paint on the palette with the leading edge slanting toward the front (see Photo 3).

PAINTING MEDIUM AND TURPENTINE: A small amount of all-purpose oil medium is placed in a clean, shallow jar, such as an empty cold cream jar, or in a small, shallow dish, such as a butter pat or tea bag holder. This container of oil is placed conveniently near the palette, where it can be easily reached while painting.

A larger jar of clean turpentine is placed near the painting medium, for cleaning brushes. Brushes should be swished through the turpentine to clean them, and must never be bounced on the bottom of the jar or jammed against its side; to do so would cause the quill to cut off some bristles, eventually ruining the brush. Baby food jars or small jam jars are excellent containers for turpentine, and can be thrown away when the turpentine becomes too dirty and oily to be of further use.

PAINTING CLOTH: A soft, lint-free cloth should be folded into a small pad of several thicknesses and placed near the painting medium and turpentine, for removing excess oil and turpentine from the brushes. As the top surface of the pad becomes soiled, it can be refolded so that a clean area is uppermost. These cloths, as well as the china silk can be cleaned by soaking them in a large jar of turpentine kept for this purpose, and then washing them in hot, soapy water.

CONDITIONING AND SHAPING BRUSHES: Square shader brushes must be conditioned and shaped before painting with them, and should be carefully cleaned and shaped after each painting session. New shader brushes are round, and the bristle ends are even; for painting, however, the hairs must be flattened and fanned out. To accomplish this, the hairs of the brush are dipped into the turpentine, then gently pressed against the painting cloth. The bristles are then dipped into the painting medium and worked back and forth on a clean area of the tile, to achieve the desired fan shape (see Photo 4). Excess oil is removed from the brush by holding it against the paint cloth while the middle finger gently presses on the ends of the hairs (see Photo 5). The brush should be conditioned often while painting, to "train" the hairs into the characteristic fan shape, and each brush should be cleaned and pressed into shape for storage.

Brushes can be stored upright, handle down, in a glass or cup — or in a flat box, providing that the hairs are not pushed out of shape by touching the end of the box. For lengthy storage, the brushes can be placed in a box with a few moth crystals or moth balls, and the edges of the box can be taped, to seal them.

LOADING THE BRUSH: When the brush has been conditioned in painting medium, has been shaped, and the excess oil has been removed, it is ready to be used. The hairs of the brush are placed on the flattened edge of one of the little piles of paint on the palette, and the brush is worked back and forth until they are evenly filled with color (see Photo 6). For shaded brushstrokes, the brush can be loaded from only one side, by placing it next to the paint and working one corner into the color with a circular motion (see Photo 7). Numerous tones of any color can be achieved by the amount of color which is picked up on the brush, and by the method used to load it. For pale tones, the color is "pulled" from the thin, front edge of the paint, while progressively deeper tones result from loading the brush farther back in the thicker areas of the paint. It should be noted that, regardless of the color tone, the coating of paint applied at any one time should be thin, to avoid blistering during the firing; successive applications of color, which are fired in between coats, are used to produce the full intensity of most colors.

PREPARING THE CHINA: China should be washed and dried, then wiped with a cloth or paper towel dampened with denatured alcohol, to be sure that it is perfectly clean and free of any grease or oil before painting.

The entire surface of the china can be tinted prior to the painting of the design, to provide a painting surface which is not as "slick" as untinted ware. China is tinted as follows: Pastel tones of colors — yellow, pink, blue or violet — are applied to the entire surface of the china, using a large brush and cross-hatch brushstrokes (see Fig. 13 of the colored brushstroke illustrations). A fist-size piece of absorbent cotton batting is then covered with the china silk, the ends of the silk being twisted to shape the cotton into a ball. One drop of painting oil is rubbed into the palm of one hand, and then the silk-covered cotton is patted on the oil-covered palm. When the silk is conditioned in this way, it is then repeatedly pounced against the china until the paint is blended into a thin, even, almost colorless film. Tinting is most readily accomplished if the cotton-covered silk is tapped smartly and rapidly against the china — a method called "pouncing." The china is then allowed to dry, and fired to cone 017. When the china is removed from the kiln, it is lightly sanded and then wiped with alcohol, to ready it for painting.

SKETCHING OR TRAC-ING ON CHINA: A design can be sketched directly onto the china with a china marking pencil, using only enough of a drawing to show placement of the design elements and omitting all details. If preferred, a design can be worked out on paper and then transferred to the china with graphite paper; commercial patterns can also be used in this way. To transfer the design with graphite paper, the graphite paper is placed, coated-side down, on the china and the pattern or sketched design is centered on top of it; the graphite paper and pattern are held in place with several small strips of masking tape. The design is then traced over, with a ball-point pen.

BRUSHSTROKES: Square shader brushes can be used to paint almost all designs, and are capable of producing an infinite number of brush-strokes. One should always use as large a brush as is possible, for the design being painted, to avoid using too many small brushstrokes. Some of the brushstrokes made with a square shader brush are illustrated here, and should be practiced until they can be made with ease. The illus-trated brushstrokes are:

FIG. A. Straight stroke

PHOTO 2

Grinding paint, with a circular motion.

PHOTO 3

Method of placing mixed
paint on palette.

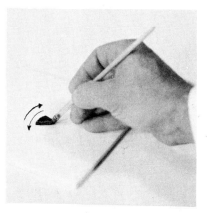

PHOTO 4

"Fanning" bristles of brush.

PHOTO 5

Pressing excess oil from brush.

PHOTO 6

Fully loading a square shader brush.

PHOTO 7

Corner loading a square shader brush.

with a fully loaded brush.

FIG. B. Cross-hatching with straight strokes. These strokes are used to apply paint for tinting blank china, and for background effects.

FIG. C. Straight strokes cross-hatching, with two colors. Any number of colors can be softly blended together in this way, with no apparent division between them. Most background colors are applied and blended in this manner.

FIG. D. "C" stroke with a fully loaded brush. The brush is pulled in a "C" shape, without turning the brush handle.

FIG. E. Comma stroke. To make this very useful stroke, the brush is placed on the china with the hairs at a 45 degree angle to the right, and then pulled down with a slight, clockwise curve.

FIGS. F & G. Figure F shows "C" strokes as they would be applied to paint a leaf, although they would actually overlap as in Figure G; a comma stroke is used to paint the tip of the leaf.

FIG. H. A shaded comma stroke. Several shaded comma strokes painted toward a central point form the basis for a flower, as shown in

Figure I. Figures J & K show this same stroke made with a small brush.

FIG. L. A "C" stroke and a reverse "C" stroke are over-lapped for the purpose of forming many flower petals. In Figure M., 5 sets of these strokes are painted toward a central point, forming the basic shape for a wild rose.

FIG. N. A dash formed by touching the hairs of a square shader brush to the painting surface. Joined end-to-end, this stroke forms tiny stems and branches.

FIG. O. A straight stroke made with a corner-loaded brush. A series of these strokes, painted end-to-end, form one side of a stem or branch; the opposite side is painted by turning the china and painting another, similar series of strokes.

FIG. P. Tiny comma strokes made with the corner of the brush. These can be used to paint rose thorns, as in Figure O.

FIG. Q. A combination of straight and comma strokes can be used to paint around design elements.

The Wild Rose

SEE COLOR PLATE 3, PAGE 9

"Wild rose" is the name given to any one of several single roses of North America — the most common being the swamp rose and the prairie rose. The swamp rose, as its name implies, is found in swamps and marshes, from Nova Scotia (in an arc) through Minnesota to the Gulf of Mexico. The prairie rose is native to eastern and central North America, from Ontario to Texas, and is most often found in scrub and open country. Similar flowers are found in Europe, the most common being the sweet briar, and in Britain where the dog rose is most often found.

All of these flowers are similar in make-up — though the leaves and fruit differ from one species to another — each one having 5 heart-shaped petals, fuzzy, yellow-tipped stamens and serrated leaves.

Wild roses are often used as an initial project for beginning painters, since the petals of these flowers are relatively large and simple when compared to other flowers, and they are fairly easy to work into a design.

It is suggested for this first project that a simple design be used, such as the one in the lower left corner of the accompanying color photo, and that it be painted on a small plate or tile. It is best — especially for these early projects — to work on a flat surface (for ease in handling), progressing to vases, pitchers, etc., once the techniques have been mastered.

White china has an extremely "slick" surface which often presents problems for beginning painters; the brush tends to slide, and it is sometimes difficult to obtain the desired depth of color in the first painting. For these reasons, it is suggested that the ware be tinted, to make the surface more pleasing to work on (see Preparing the China, Chapter 2). When the china has been tinted and fired, it should be lightly sanded with the fine sandpaper and then wiped with an alcohol-dampened cloth or paper towel.

The following instructions for sketching and painting wild roses should be practiced until each part can be painted with ease. Do not hesitate to wipe off and repaint any part, or all of the design, as often as is necessary.

Use a china-marking pencil to sketch the design onto the prepared china. A wild rose blossom can be compared in shape to a champagne glass with the base broken off (see the drawing), the container part of the glass corresponding to the petal portion of the flower and the stem of the glass corresponding to the calyx and stem of the flower. The drawings show a wild rose superimposed on a champagne glass, each one in a slightly different position. Thinking of the flower as a glass shape makes it easy to sketch wild roses in any position. The same type of association will be helpful when sketching leaves, stems and buds; as illustrated in the drawings, a leaf can be compared to the back of a spoon, stems resemble pieces of soda straw, and buds are comprised of a cone and 2 ball shapes.

It is not necessary to include in the sketch the details, such as stamens and the serrated leaf edges, since they will not be painted for the first firing.

When the design is sketched onto the china, it must be decided from which direction within the scene the light will come; as a rule, this is either the upper left or upper right. Once a light source has been established, it must be maintained throughout the various applications of color which lead to a finished painting. It may be helpful to pencil a small "X" on the china, as a reminder of the direction from which the light is coming; this mark can be replaced after each firing. The light source will, of course, determine where shadows will fall within the design, and which of the design elements will be highlighted. Careful use of light

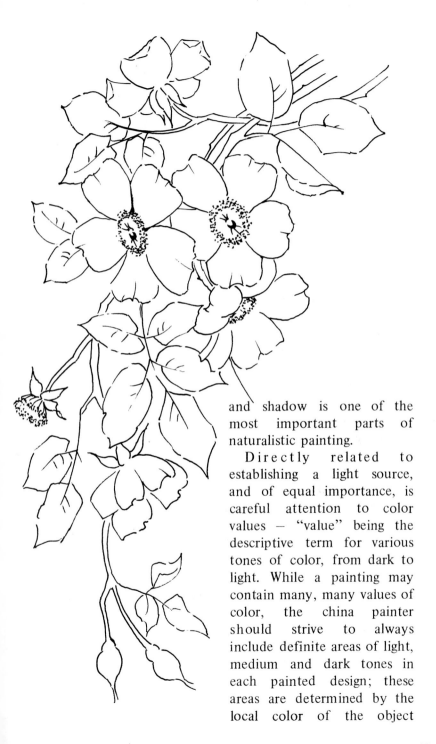

and shadow is one of the most important parts of naturalistic painting.

Directly related to establishing a light source, and of equal importance, is careful attention to color values — "value" being the descriptive term for various tones of color, from dark to light. While a painting may contain many, many values of color, the china painter should strive to always include definite areas of light, medium and dark tones in each painted design; these areas are determined by the local color of the object being rendered, and the amount of light falling upon it. Dark color accents near a design — whether in background or foliage colors — tend to "lift" the design above them, and intensify the 3-dimensional, naturalistic effect.

FIRST PAINTING

Condition a #10 square shader brush as directed in Chapter 2, and fully load it with pale pink. Paint the flower petals with this color, using only one or 2 strokes for each one. Paint the center of each flower with mixing yellow, allowing this color to blend into the base of the petals; do not paint the centers of these flowers as round spots of color.

Wash over the leaves with yellow green, being sure to leave a large highlight (unpainted area) on each leaf. Use yellow green and a little brown green, mixed on the brush, to paint the buds and to do the calyx of the blown flower.

Surround the entire design with background colors, using yellow green, yellow green and blue mixed on the brush, blue and yellow. Keep these background colors light in tone, and blend them into

one another so that there are no definite lines between colors. Gently blend some of the background color over the flower edges, so that these edges are soft, elusive and somewhat transparent in appearance.

Using a piece of china silk over a finger, or a clean oil-conditioned brush, wipe large highlights from the flower petals (see the color photo).

This first painting should be fairly light in tone, and the design elements surrounded by background should have "soft" edges. Much shaping and refining will be done on subsequent paintings, but it can only be done successfully if the first painting has no sharp, defined edges.

Fire the piece to cone 017, and sand it lightly when it has been removed from the kiln.

SECOND PAINTING

Using black green, blue and mixing yellow, for background colors, deepen the background around the design, paying special attention to the "corners" between petals and leaves. Use these background colors to give the flowers their final shape.

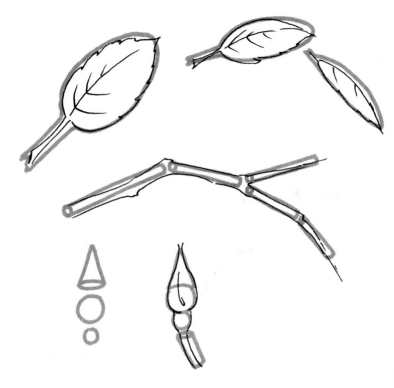

Corner-load the shader brush with dark pink, and use it to deepen the color of the petals near the flower centers and to indicate the separations between petals. Clean and condition the brush, and softly "feather" the dark pink into the unpainted parts of the petals.

Corner-load the shader brush with yellow brown light, and, with a "C"-shaped stroke, darken one side of each flower center. Paint a small "C" stroke of olive green in the middle of each flower center, to represent the tightly packed anthers which form the little "button" in the center of a wild rose. Load the liner brush with yellow brown dark, and paint a series of dots around the center, simulating the ends of the stamens; add a few dots of dark brown. Allow these dots to dry for a few minutes, then use a brush handle to "knock out" many seed-like spots among the dots. Paint a few lines of rich brown from the green center button to the ring of dots.

Use olive green, brown green and black green for the

leaves, being sure to allow some of the original color to show. Use a clean brush to wipe a few veins in the leaves (see the color photo), but do not define every vein in every leaf, or the leaves will detract from the flowers. Where leaves seem to overlap one another, paint each leaf as if it stands alone, then use a clean, conditioned brush to wipe a highlight from the "top" leaf; this will immediately make one leaf advance and the other recede, and is much easier than trying to paint dark shadows on the underleaves.

Darken the shadow sides of stems and buds, with brown green and a little violet of iron. Use the same colors on any calyxes which show under blossoms.

Paint the "seedy" mass of stamens on has-beens — flowers which have dropped their petals — with an oval of dots, as in the flower centers.

Allow the painting to dry; then fire the piece to cone 017.

THIRD PAINTING

Sand the piece, and wipe it with alcohol.

Add sharp accents of dark pink to the flowers, and heighten the "cupped" effect of some petals by washing a little yellow green over their center areas. Use the liner brush to paint tiny, triangular-shaped "spaces" between some of the petals. For flowers which are under (and shadowed by) other flowers, wash over the petals with a little black green, to make them appear to recede (painting over any color with its complementary will gray the original color, making it appear to drop back in space).

Darken the shadow areas of the leaves with brown green and violet of iron, mixed on the brush. Paint tiny touches of violet of iron along the leaf edges, to simulate the serrated edges which wild rose leaves have. Use the brown green-violet of iron mixture to accent the stems, buds and calyxes.

Deepen the background colors in the "corners" around the design, especially on the shadow side.

Be sure, in this final painting, that no part of the design is completely covered with paint, as this could cause the entire painting to "go flat" and thereby lose its 3-dimensional quality. This third painting should be used only to add accents of color.

Fire the piece again to cone 017.

Violets on China

SEE COLOR PLATE 4, PAGE 10

Violets, long-time favorites of china painters, are members of the VIOLA family, which is comprised of between 4 and 5 hundred members. These hardy plants thrive throughout much of Europe, North America, South America, Africa and Asia – and one particularly sturdy variety is at home in the Arctic, where it bears pale, almost white blossoms. Here, in the United States, the bird's foot and other common violets are the most prolific of the wild varieties, while the sweet violet is the most popular cultivated type. One violet, the viola alba, is cultivated in the Middle East, or its perfume.

While violets come in many colors, the most familiar are those which have petals of blue-purple, with a spurred lower petal, 5 green sepals and heart-shaped leaves.

The structure of violet blossoms is very much like that of pansies – a close relative – having 2 top, 2 side and one lower petal. The side petals have a patch of fuzzy stamens where they join in the center of the flower, and these stamens form the characteristic "tent" which frames the lower petal. Some varieties have dark patches of "whiskers" on the side and lower petals, another indication that they belong to the same family as pansies.

The following instructions are for sketching and painting violets, buds, partially opened flowers and leaves.

Tint the china, as described in Chapter 2; then fire it. Lightly sand the tinted surface of the fired piece, and wipe it with a cloth dampened in denatured alcohol.

SKETCHING THE DESIGN

Use a china marking pencil to sketch the design onto the china. A violet blossom is basically round, with 5 equally spaced petals which would compare to the points of a star (see the drawings, which show a violet superimposed on a star within a circle, each one in a slightly different position). Buds are basically elongated diamond shapes, and partially opened flowers are basically cone shapes. It is not necessary, of course, to draw the geometric figures, but one should keep these shapes in mind while sketching the design; consequently, each part will have the correct form.

Omit all details from the pencil sketch, such as whiskers and leaf veins, since they will not be painted for the first fire.

Decide from which direction within the scene the light will come, so that highlights and shadows can be placed correctly.

FIRST PAINTING

Condition a #6 shader brush as directed in Chapter 2, and load it with dark purple; pick up a little pale blue on the same brush (since violets come in different colors and tones of colors, the purple and blue can

be mixed on the brush so tha whichever one is desired wi predominate). On each of th top and side petals, pull comma stroke toward the flowe center, leaving their outer edge free of color.

Load the brush with dar purple and use comma stroke to fill in the spaces between th main flowers in the design. Pair loose comma strokes around th group of flowers, to give th illusion of more blossoms be hind them. Clean and conditio the brush, then use it to wip out the "tent" at the center c each flower, and the area on th large petal directly under it. Fi the wiped-out area on the larg petals with mixing yellow.

Wash over the leaves wit yellow green, leaving large high lights along one side of each c the center vein; paint th calyxes on the buds with th same color. Surround the desig with cross-hatch strokes of blu some of purple and blue mixe on the brush, some of blac green, and some of mixin yellow. Be sure to softly feathe one background color into ai other, to avoid definite lines c separation between them. Use sharpened brush handle, or wooden meat skewer, to wip out the stems.

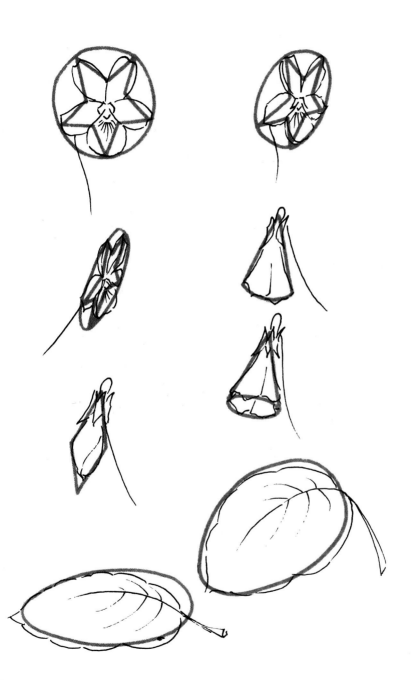

Allow the painting to dry, and fire the piece to cone 017; then sand it lightly.

SECOND PAINTING

Deepen the background colors around the design, paying special attention to the "corners" formed by the joining of petals and leaves. Corner-load the brush with dark purple, and use this to accent the spaces between the flowers.

Deepen the color in the centers of the flowers, avoiding the highlights at the petal edges and the white tents. Be sure that at this time there are definite areas of light, medium and dark ones in the flowers, to avoid a "flat" look.

Shape each leaf with brown green, beginning at one edge and drawing the brush toward the center vein; then shade the opposite edge, but do not pull the color all of the way to the vein lines. Allow the leaves to dry for a few minutes, then use clean, oil-conditioned brush to wipe out a few side veins. Use the corner of the brush to accent the calyxes with brown green and to sketch in the stems. Pull the corner of a clean, oil-conditioned brush down the length of each stem, to highlight and give it a rounded look.

Allow the painting to dry; then fire the piece to cone 017.

THIRD PAINTING

Lightly sand the piece, and wipe it with denatured alcohol.

Add sharp accents of purple to the flowers, then use the same color and a liner brush to paint the whiskers on the lower petal of only 2 or 3 of the violets. Corner-load the shader brush with Persian red, and paint a tiny comma stroke under each white tent area.

Darken the shadow areas on the leaves, with black green, for the very deep shadow areas; where the leaves are tucked under the flowers, use black green and a little purple, mixed on the brush.

Fire the piece again, to cone 017.

Pansies on China

SEE COLOR PLATE 5, PAGE 11

Pansies, the heartsease of ancient days (one of the oldest of cultivated flowers), have been loved by gardeners for centuries; John Parkinson, writing in 1629, mentions heartsease, and Milton calls it "pansy freak'ed with jet." Over the years, this lovely, colorful blossom has been known by many names, some of them being: Tittle-my-Fancy, Kiss-me-at-the-Garden-Gate and Love-in-Idleness. The pansies of today are believed to be derived from the viola tricolor, a common weed of European fields, but bear small resemblance to their tiny ancestor.

Like their closest relative, violets, pansies have 5 petals, the lower one being spurred and all of them overlapping. Perhaps the best known characteristic of pansies is the distinct pattern which marks the side and lower petals of each blossom, accenting the "tent" at their joining point.

Pansies are a joy to paint, because of the many colors and color combinations which can be used. While the ancestor of these flowers has 2 petals of purple and 3 of pale lavender blue, the pansies of today bloom in literally hundreds of color tones, ranging from pale, creamy yellow to deep red brown, and from white to rich, royal purple; quite often, the 2 back petals will be one color, while the side and lower petals will be an entirely different color. The blossoms are basically round and flat in shape, the 3 lower petals being the most prominent, with the 2 top petals just peeking above them.

While pansies are a joy to paint, it is a challenge to paint them realistically. It is vital to the success of the painting to pay special attention to highlights while forming the ruffled petals; to ignore this important point will cause the painted flowers to appear flat and uninteresting. When planning a pansy design, it is also recommended that reference be made to good photos and color studies of pansies, as well as to actual flowers, when available. Just as it is more difficult to paint a likeness of a baby than of an older person, much more attention must be given to "simple" flowers, where light, shadow and color must be carefully rendered to bring a feeling of realness and life to the painting.

will become eliptical as it turns toward or away from the viewer (the flowers in the accompanying design have been superimposed on circular and oval shapes, to illustrate this point).

The directions which follow are for the pansies pictured in the lower right of the color photo, while the remaining sections of the photo show the color buildup and modeling achieved in 3 separate paintings. Practice painting this small design with the colors given, then paint others with colors and color combinations of your choosing.

PREPARATION

Tint the blank china with any pale color or colors, then fire and sand it. Wipe the tinted china with an alcohol-dampened cloth or paper towel.

Use the china marking pencil to sketch the design onto the prepared china. As stated previously, pansies are basically round in shape, so circular shapes can be used as the basis for the design; remember that for flowers viewed from other than straight on, the circular shape

FIRST PAINTING

Condition a #10 square shader brush, as directed in Chapter 2, and fully load it with mixing yellow. Paint the 3 lower petals of the main flower with this color, leaving unpainted areas between brushstrokes, to achieve a ruffled effect on the petal edges. Pick up a little yellow brown on the corner of the brush, and paint the "throat" of the lower petal. Clean the brush and condition it in oil, then use the corner of it to clean the color from the patch of anthers on each side petal to form the tent over the

throat. Load the brush with pale violet and paint the 2 back petals, once again leaving highlights to obtain a ruffled effect. Paint the partially open flower at the upper left of the design, with these same colors.

Paint the 3 lower petals of the remaining flower, with pale violet and dark blue mixed together on the brush. Use yellow brown for the throat on the lower petal. Mix pale violet and dark blue on the brush, using slightly more blue than violet, and paint the 2 back petals; paint the closed bud with these same colors.

Wash over the leaves and the calyxes with yellow green, leaving large areas unpainted on the leaves, for highlights.

Surround the design with background colors, using black green, blue and yellow. Blend these colors together where they meet, so that there are no definite lines between them. Gently blend some of the background colors over the flower edges, so that the petal edges have a soft, somewhat transparent look. Use a sharpened brush handle, or a meat skewer, to wipe out the stems.

This first painting should be light in tone, with no "hard" edges.

Fire the piece to cone 017, and sand it lightly when it has been removed from the kiln.

SECOND PAINTING

Deepen the background colors around the design, and use these colors to further shape the flowers wherever necessary. Pay particular attention to the spaces formed between leaves and flowers and between leaves and stems, making these areas dark, to give a feeling of depth.

Corner-load the shader brush with yellow brown, and shade the yellow side petals of the main flower, to heighten the effect of separation between them and the lower petal. Lightly accent the edges of the yellow petals with yellow brown, to further add to the ruffled appearance. Shade the top petals of this flower with purple and dark blue, mixed together on the brush. Shade the partially open flower, in the same way.

Accent the remaining flower with touches of purple and dark blue, to separate the petals and increase the ruffled effect of the petal edges.

Shade and model the leaves with brown green and a little black green. Refine the calyxes on the partially open flower and the bud, with brown green. Paint the stems brown green, then draw the corner of a clean, conditioned brush along each stem, to give it a rounded appearance.

Fire the piece to cone 017.

THIRD PAINTING

For this painting, do not completely cover any area with color, since to do so could cause the painting to loose its 3-dimensional quality. Add only sharp accents of color to the flower petals, using yellow brown on the yellow petals and purple and dark blue on the violet ones. Using a mixture of purple and ruby on the liner brush, paint the patches on the lower 3 petals of each flower. Paint a touch of this color mixture under each side of the tent, to make it appear as if a pistol is protruding from the center of each lower petal.

Add a little very dark color to the background, in "corners" formed by the joining of leaves and petals. Deepen the color on the leaves, if necessary.

Fire the piece again, to cone 017.

Color and Color Management

SEE COLOR PLATE 6, PAGE 12

Man has been attracted and fascinated by color since prehistoric times, and has used it to decorate his person, his home and his possessions in numerous ways. Those of us who are in any way connected with the decorative arts share the same interest in color which intrigued our remote ancestors in the dawn of time.

Color as a subject for study is amazingly complex, involving sciences such as chemistry, physiology, psychology and physics. And, while it is not necessary for the hobbyist to delve into a detailed study, basic knowledge will aid in the selection and use of color.

It had been observed that a beam of light passing through a prism produced the familiar colors of the solar spectrum, but it was not until 1666 that a serious study of the phenomenon was undertaken, by Sir Isaac Newton. Since that time, many others have advanced the knowledge of color and the part that it plays in our lives. The results of the years of experimentation by dedicated men are the basis for our knowledge of color.

COLOR DIMENSIONS

Color has 3 dimensions: hue, intensity and value.

Hue, the first dimension, is what distinguishes one color from another and identifies it by name; i.e., yellow, blue, green, violet, etc.

Intensity, the second dimension, can be simply stated as the relative brightness of a color's hue.

Value, color's third dimension, establishes its relative position to white and black. At their full intensity, colors such as yellow, yellow orange and yellow green are high in value (nearer to white), while red, blue and purple are low in value (nearer to black).

Understanding the dimensions of any color is important to the china painter, since the proper application of all color is necessary in order to properly select color combinations, realistically render form and add depth in painting. Of the 3 dimensions, value is the most important for the china painter to understand and to put to use in painting; without the correct application of value, paintings will lack contrast and like life quality. Objects within a painting that are in the path of light should be higher in value (lighter) than those which receive less light, such as those in shadow. Light colors can be made to appear even lighter by placing them against dark colors, while dark colors will appear even darker by placing them against light colors. To be successful, any painting must contain areas of color value ranging from light to dark, relative to the overall intensity of the colors used.

The value of any color can be changed — made lighter or darker — by the addition of white, black and/or other colors. When white is added to any color, lightening its value, the resultant color is called a "tint"; colors darkened by the addition of black or a darker color of the same general hue are called "shades." Since white china paint is very seldom used (being an opacifier), tints of china paints are simply obtained by applying the colors more thinly, allowing the white of the china to optically reduce the value of the color being applied.

THE COLOR WHEEL

The solar spectrum, which has red at one end and violet at the other, is bent into a circle and joined with red violet (which does not appear in the spectrum), to form a color wheel (see Figure 1); this is the accepted method of diagramming colors and their relationships to one another. The 12 colors on a color wheel are: primary colors — red, yellow and blue; secondary colors — orange, violet and green; and intermediate colors — yellow green, blue green, blue violet, red violet, red orange and yellow orange.

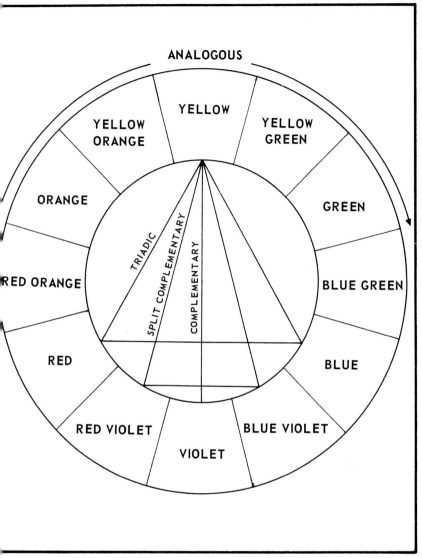

FIGURE 1

The primary colors are those which cannot be produced by mixtures of other colors, yet can themselves be mixed to form all other colors. Secondary colors are placed on the color wheel equidistant between the 2 primary colors which are mixed to produce them. Intermediate colors are positioned between the primary and secondary colors, and can be produced by mixing those colors.

Colors diametrically opposite one another on the color wheel are known as "complementary," and mixtures of these colors are tertiary colors. Browns and other earth colors fall into this category, since they are formed by the mixture of the red and orange colors and their complementaries.

COLOR HARMONY

While selection of a color scheme for a painting depends a great deal upon personal preference, there are four methods of choosing colors which have pleasing relationships with one another. The 4 most often used color harmonies are: direct complementary, split complementary, triadic and analogous. The color wheel can be used as a visual aid to select pleasing color harmonies for any type of painting (see Figure 1).

Complementary harmony consists of any 2 colors diametrically opposite each other on the color wheel, and their tints and shades.

Split complementary harmony is a color and the colors on either side of its complementary; i.e., yellow, blue violet and red violet or green, red

violet and red orange.

Triadic harmony is composed of any 3 colors which fall at the points of an equilateral triangle placed on the color wheel; i.e., orange, violet and green.

Analogous harmony consists of any 5 contiguous colors on the color wheel and their tints and shades. The rule for this color harmony is that one of the primary colors must be in all 5 colors used i.e., orange, yellow orange, yellow, yellow green and green.

Another harmony, which is not indicated on the color wheel in figure one, is monochromatic. This harmony is simply various values and intensities of any single color.

Tertiary colors and their tints and shades are, along with black and white, considered to be neutral; and, therefore, harmonize with all colors and color harmonies.

MIXING COLORS

Theoretically, a painter would need only red, yellow and blue pigments, from which he would be able to mix all other colors; unfortunately, this procedure does not always work in actual practice, and the painter must rely to a great extent on the range of commercial colors available. It is, however, possible to select a palette of a limited number of colors, and from it mix innumerable other colors — enough to cover any situation.

The color palette suggested in Chapter 1 should, with the physical mixture of colors and necessary gray tones, enable the china painter to portray any subject. To produce gray tones of a color, essential for any successful painting, it is only necessary to mix it with its complementary color, such as red with green, violet with yellow, etc. Some very useful gray tones can be mixed, such as brown green and violet of iron, dark blue and yellow brown, dark blue and rich brown, ruby and black green; any color can also be grayed by the addition of black, but the effect is usually less interesting. It is suggested that some time be spent in trying physical mixtures of the colors on the palette; these mixtures can be applied to tiles and fired, then stored for future reference, or formulas for the most pleasing mixtures can be recorded in a notebook.

Because china paints are transparent, it is possible to obtain even more colors by applying one color over another color which has been fired; colors produced in this way will be different than the mixture of the same 2 colors before firing. To see the effect of colors applied over other fired colors, a series of tiles can be prepared (see the color photo); this can be easily retained, for instant reference. To prepare such a color chart, proceed as follows:

Mix some black china paint powder with enough sugar water, Coca Cola, 7 Up, or corn syrup thinned with water, to produce an "ink" thin enough to flow from a dip pen (when dry, this "ink" is not affected by painting oil or turpentine, so it can be used to draw and write on china whenever black outlines are desired). Place 4 tiles in a square and, using a ruler, mark off 24 horizontal and vertical sections each 3/8" wide. Write or print one color name at the end of each horizontal row, then repeat the same color names in the same order at the end of the vertical rows. Apply a wash of the indicated color to each horizontal row.

Allow the tiles to dry, then fire them to cone 017. Lightly sand the tiles, and return them to their original positions. Next, apply a wash of the indicated color to each vertical row, and allow the color to dry. Fire the tiles to cone 017, then mount them in correct order, on a piece of plywood. This "plaid" tile will indicate the resultant colors when any one color has been painted over all other fired colors contained on the palette.

Another visual aid which can be helpful to the china painter is an indication of what effect successive applications of the same color will have. This chart (see color photo) can be prepared, as follows:

Using the ink described above, divide a plate into 24 equal, wedge-shaped sections.

Print the name of a color at the edge of the plate in each section. Apply a wash of the indicated color to each entire section. Fire and sand the plate. Apply the same color to each section, covering only 2/3 of the plate from the center out. Fire and sand the plate. Apply the same colors to the sections, covering only the center 1/3 of the plate. Fire.

As stated earlier, the study of color can be most complex, and most hobbyists would not care to devote the time necessary to such a study; however, experimenting with color and color mixtures as described above can be rewarding and pleasurable when applied to china painting.

Forget-Me Nots

SEE COLOR PLATE 7, PAGE 13

Forget-me-nots are represented in the United States by some dozen native species of an almost world-wide family of more than forty. The genus name of these flowers – "Myosotis" – is from the Greek words "my" (mouse) and "otos" (ear), for the shapes of the leaves. Several romantic legends are credited with the popular name "forget-me-not," the most prevalent being one of German origin. This tale tells of a drowning knight's last words to his lady, when he slipped into the water while gathering flowers for her. An even earlier name for forget-me-nots was "scorpion grass," because the curled flower stems were thought to resemble a scorpion's tail.

China painters have long been attracted by these dainty little flowers, using them in designs by themselves and in conjunction with other flowers. The blue variety of forget-me-nots (there are also pink ones and white ones) being one of the few, true blue blossoms, are perfect foils for pink wild roses, pink roses and white flowers such as daisies.

Since the flowers of forget-me-nots are borne on leafless stems which emerge from the base of leaves on the main plant stem, the painter must exercise artistic license in order to gracefully incorporate leaves into a design. The flower stems continue to grow the full length of the blooming period, as buds – which are pink – develop at the very ends of the stems. The flowers themselves have 5 fairly round petals, arranged in a saucer shape around a yellow center.

The calyxes are cone shaped, and are connected to the flower stem by a short stem. The flowers are so arranged on the flower stems that they form clusters along the upper side of a main stem. The leaves of the forget-me-not are light green in color, and are rather long in shape, with clearly defined center veins and fairly blunt tips.

To digress from the subject for a moment, the mention of leaves brings to mind something of a fault of which many painters — advanced as well as beginners — are often guilty. It is not uncommon, when viewing a display of painted china, to form an opinion that all flora used as subject matter have exactly the same type of leaves; and, more often than not, they are leaves which would be at home only on rose bushes! An easy trap to fall into is that of learning to paint one type of leaf and then using it for every kind of flower and fruit. Many leaves are similar in shape, but the difference in leaves from one plant to another should be noted and then incorporated into each painting. There are many books, studies and

photographs, which portray all types of plants realistically, that can be used for reference when planning a design; and, when available, the actual plant should be studied. Every painter seriously interested in improving his skill should have a sketchbook wherein sketches and notes may be kept (see black and white photo for an example of such a sketchbook). The sketches need not be extremely detailed, but should show each flower in various stages of development and in various positions, as well as showing the appropriate leaves — their general shape, and how they are attached to the stem or branch. Constant reference to studies and sketchbook before and during painting sessions will assure that the correct leaf will always be used for each type of flower and fruit.

While real forget-me-nots usually have only 3 to 5 open flowers per cluster, they are often painted in larger clusters, for a more pleasing effect. Forget-me-nots, and other flowers which grow in clusters, such as lilacs, snowballs, lantanas, etc., are often easiest to portray by the

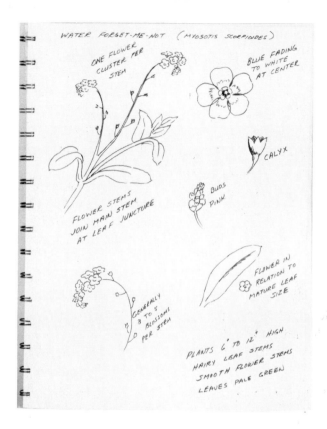

WATER FORGET-ME-NOT (MYOSOTIS SCORPIOIDES)

ONE FLOWER CLUSTER PER STEM

BLUE FADING TO WHITE AT CENTER

CALYX

BUDS PINK

FLOWER STEMS JOIN MAIN STEM AT LEAF JUNCTURE

GENERALLY 3 TO 5 BLOSSOMS PER STEM

FLOWER IN RELATION TO MATURE LEAF SIZE

PLANTS 6" TO 12" HIGH
HAIRY LEAF STEMS
SMOOTH FLOWER STEMS
LEAVES PALE GREEN

wiping-out method, which has not as yet been covered in previous chapters. The wiping-out method is not only useful for flowers which grow in clusters, but can be used for painting groups or clusters of other flowers, such as violets and daisies, and for fruits, such as grapes, currants and raspberries. One of the main differences between the wiping-out process and other methods of china painting is that the initial sketch is either omitted or is put in with india ink; a pencil sketch would be destroyed by painting over it, while india ink will not be affected. For the step-by-step, color photos which accompany this article, an india ink sketch was used.

PREPARATION

Tint the china with pale pink, then fire and sand it. Wipe the tinted china with an alcohol-dampened cloth or paper towel.

Use the china-marking pencil to sketch the design onto the prepared china, or trace it on with graphite paper. Now, using a dip pen with a fine point and india ink, go over all of the design outlines. Allow the inked design to dry, then wipe the piece with a cloth dampened with turpentine; the turpentine will remove the pencil or graphite marks, but it will not affect the inked lines, and the india ink will burn off in the first firing.

The upper left section of the color photo shows a group of wiped-out flowers before the piece is fired for the first time; the india ink outlines are clearly discernible.

FIRST PAINTING

Corner-load a #10 shader brush with pale blue, and paint a series of small "C" strokes over the entire flower area. Then corner-load the same brush with dark blue, and use it to fill in all open areas in the flower area between the pale blue strokes.

Surround the flower area with background colors of yellow, pale pink and black green. Softly feather the background colors into the blue of the flower area and into each other, so that there are no hard, dividing lines between any of the colors.

Dampen the #4 shader brush in turpentine, then press the brush firmly against the paint cloth, to remove as much as possible of the turpentine. (Pay special attention to this step since any appreciable amount of turpentine transferred to the china by the brush will cause the paint to "bleed," or run.) With the brush prepared in this manner, and reconditioning it as often as is necessary, carefully wipe the paint from all of the leaves and outlined flowers. In addition to the outlined blossoms, wipe out a few petal shapes within the blue, flower area; in the finished painting, these extra wipe-outs will give the impression of other blossoms peeking from behind the main flowers.

Paint the leaves and main stems yellow green, leaving large highlights on the leaves.

Fire the piece to cone 017, then sand it and wipe it with an alcohol-dampened cloth (the upper right section of the color photo shows the piece after the first firing).

SECOND PAINTING

Deepen the color around

the wiped-out flowers, using dark blue; then use a mixture of dark blue and dark yellow brown to darken the deeply shadowed areas. Gently pull some of these colors into the background areas, using small strokes to represent shadow flowers.

Paint all of the wiped-out petals with pale blue, leaving a small area unpainted in the center of each flower. Clean and condition the brush in oil, then wipe out the petals of those flowers which are to appear to overlap or be on top of other flowers. Paint the center of each flower, with mixing yellow.

Using yellow green, olive green and a little brown green, paint the leaves, being sure to define the center vein of each one. Paint the stems with a mixture of brown green and yellow green.

Touch the base of each tiny bud with a little dark pink, then use a liner brush to add to each one a calyx of brown green.

Darken the background colors, where necessary, paying special attention to the shadow (lower left) side of the design.

Fire the piece to cone 017, then sand it and wipe it with an alcohol-dampened cloth.

THIRD PAINTING

For this third painting, do not completely cover any area with color; use only the minimum amount of paint necessary to heighten the 3-dimensional effect.

Accent the "corners" between flower petals, and refine the shapes of any ragged petals, with a touch of dark blue. Wash over the center portions of the lightest petals with a little turquoise, to produce a "cupped" effect; use turquoise color sparingly, since it is extremely strong. Paint a tiny dot of rich brown in the middle of each flower center. On a few of the dominant flowers, add a touch of dark yellow brown to one side of the center.

Deepen the color on the leaves in only the shadow areas, using brown green and a little black green.

Fire the piece to cone 017.

Applying Gold

Many pieces of painted china can be enhanced by the judicious addition of gold accents; indeed, some china, because of its shape, decorative edges and handles, would seem incomplete without gleaming touches of gold. While other metals — platinum, silver and palladium — are also used to decorate china, gold has always been, and still is, preferred by most painters. Quite often, a narrow band of gold around the edge of a painted plate will make the difference between a piece that is attractive and one that is outstanding. However, the indiscriminate use of gold should be avoided, and the painter's own good taste must be followed to assure a pleasant balance between the painted design and the gold accents.

Gold, or any other metallic accent, should be used only to complement the painted design and should, therefore, always remain subordinate to it. The beginning painter is advised to carefully plan where and if gold would really add to the beauty of a piece of china, rather than haphazardly applying it to every piece that is painted.

Gold is available in several forms, the most often used by china painters being "burnish" and "liquid bright."

BURNISH GOLD

Burnish gold is also known as coin, Roman and paste, and is the one which produces a soft, satiny finish. Burnish gold is pure gold which has been chemically transformed into fine powder. Although available as a powder, this gold is more familiar to china painters in paste form — the result of its being mixed with various oils. Paste burnish gold is available in pats (on small, glass slabs) and in jars in larger amounts, such as 1/8, 1/4 and 1/2 ounces.

There are three types of burnish gold: fluxed, unfluxed and liquid, the first two being the most commonly used. In addition, these materials are available in various gold colors, such as green gold, red gold, etc.

Many beginning painters are confused as to when to use regular (fluxed) burnish gold and when to use unfluxed gold, some believing that they are actually different materials. Both are the same, real gold, but one has flux added to it so that it will unite during the gold firing with the fired glaze that is already on the piece. Unfluxed gold is to be applied over fired china colors, and, as the paints have sufficient flux to assure the adherence of the gold, no additional flux is necessary. The thing to be remembered is that fluxed gold should be applied to plain china, and unfluxed gold should be used over fired color.

Unfired burnish gold is dark brown in color, and derives its name from the fact that it must be burnished, or polished, after it has been fired, to achieve the sheen of real gold.

When a piece of china decorated with gold is removed from the kiln, the gold will be dull yellow with a frosted appearance. Fired gold must not be touched with the hands before it is polished, since the oils from the skin can cause marks which cannot be burnished away and the piece would have to be fired again to remove them. Fired gold can be burnished with burnishing sand, glass brushes or tape, agate burnishers, spun glass insulating material and spun glass pads. Burnishing sand does the best job and is simple to use, being applied with a damp cloth, but a glass brush is often useful to burnish hard-to-reach areas.

Burnish gold in paste form, whether in pat or bulk, is too thick to be used as is, so it must be conditioned for use, with the proper thinner or medium. Commercially prepared facilitator, lavender oil or turpentine can be used as a medium, facilitator and lavender oil being preferred; turpentine dries too rapidly, and, after repeated use, causes the gold to become sticky. The constant use of turpentine is also often believed to be the cause of blisters in fired gold, due to the fat left by evaporation.

Because burnish gold is real gold, it is expensive (prices fluctuating with the gold market), care should be practiced in its preparation and application. Even though a painter uses enough gold to require its purchase in bulk form, a pat consisting of a small glass slab in a box with a cover should be kept on hand for mixing the gold for application, to avoid waste. In addition, a separate palette knife for use exclusively with gold will prove economical, since it need not be cleaned — thus wasting gold — after each use.

To prepare burnish gold for application, a few drops of the medium are placed on it on the glass slab, and it is allowed to stand for a few minutes, to soften it; gold purchased in pats often becomes very hard, and requires additional "softening" time. When the gold has softened, it is worked with the palette knife, with, if necessary, additional medium to bring it to the consistency of heavy cream; GOLD MUST NOT BE OVERTHINNED.

Gold is NEVER mixed by "stirring" it with a brush; this would not only be wasteful, but invariably bristles from the brush would be broken off and mixed into the gold. The gold is turned over with the knife to mix it, and occasionally turned again as work progresses, since the medium will work to the top as the mixture stands.

The correct application of burnish gold is something that must be learned by practice. When applied too thinly (usually the result of trying to "stretch" the gold for the sake of economy), the gold may rub off during the burnishing process, resulting in bare or streaked areas. When gold is applied too heavily, the painter is taking the risk that it will blister during the firing; such blisters can be covered by another coat of gold only after the flaws have been sanded down. A good criterion of correct applications is the "feel" of the material as it is being applied; gold that has been excessively thinned will flow on smoothly and perhaps run, while gold which is too thick will not spread but will feel stiff and sticky. When correctly conditioned, the gold will go on smoothly, with just a bit of resistance to being brushed out.

A small, square shader, quill brush and a liner brush should be reserved for the application of burnish gold; for painting scrolls (to be covered in a later chapter), a long-bristled brush, called a "scroller," is also necessary. These brushes should be kept separate from other painting supplies, and reserved for the application of burnish gold. For the sake of economy, frequently used brushes for burnish gold need not be cleaned after every use, providing that· the gold is not allowed to dry on the bristles. Brushes containing gold will stay soft for some time, if they are dipped in medium and then stored in an air-tight container, such as a test tube or a glass cigar container tightly capped or corked. Some painters fashion a storage container for each gold brush, by drilling a hole in the lid of· a small bottle into which the brush handle will fit snuggly. The brush handle is forced through this hole from the inside of the cap, so that when the cap is screwed onto the container the bristles of the brush are above the bottom of the bottle (see the drawing).

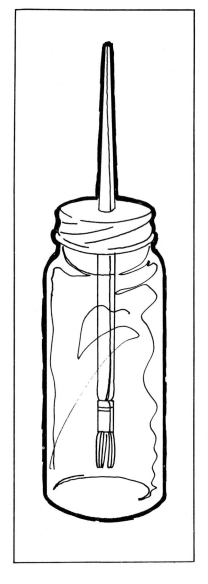

To assure that the bottle is air tight, glue is applied around the brush handle and allowed to dry. With this arrangement, the lid is not removed from the brush when it is used.

If, however, brushes for burnish gold are used only occasionally, they should be cleaned after each use. Brushes to be cleaned should be dipped into medium, then pressed onto the glass slab, to remove and save as much of the gold as possible. The brushes should then be washed in a small jar of alcohol until clean, and then pressed against a soft cloth to dry. The same jar of alcohol should be used whenever a brush containing burnish gold is to be cleaned; the gold will settle to the bottom of the jar, and, when enough is accumulated, the alcohol can be allowed to evaporate and the gold residue reclaimed. This reclaimed gold can then be mixed with some medium and used as a first coat (undercoat) for burnish gold.

Burnish gold can be fired at regular china firing temperatures.

LIQUID BRIGHT GOLD

The main use of liquid bright gold — which is really a lustre — is as an undercoat for the more expensive burnish gold. Liquid bright gold, when fired, has a brassy look, which does not complement painted china; if used at all for a finish coat, it should be applied with the greatest restraint.

Liquid bright gold can be added in small amounts to burnish gold, for the sake of economy, since it does make burnish gold "go farther"; however, this should be done cautiously, since too much liquid bright gold will cause the burnish gold to turn brassy.

It is very easy to apply liquid bright gold, as any unevenness of application disappears in the firing. This gold can be used without any special preparation, just as it comes from the bottle; the only difficulty which might be encountered is that of unexpected spreading, if too much is used. Many painters prefer to pour a few drops of liquid bright gold onto a tile, or a small glass slab, to allow it to thicken slightly by evaporation before application to china.

Since this gold is liquid, it can be applied with a pen, for fine scrolling, lettering and writing and other line work. When applied over fired china paint, liquid bright loses its brassy look and is similar in appearance to burnish gold;

for this reason, fine scrolling of liquid bright over fired color is an acceptable method of decoration.

The chief caution which must be observed in the use of liquid bright gold is the prevention of smears, which, even though invisible on unfired china, will result in ugly, purple blotches when the piece is fired. Whenever it is necessary to remove unfired liquid bright gold from a piece of china, it first should be wiped off with a clean piece of cotton batting dampened in alcohol; the cotton should be discarded after use, to avoid transferring the gold on it to other china. If a purple smear does appear on a piece of fired china (it is quite often found on the backs of pieces, having been transferred there by the fingers), it can be removed with commercially available gold remover, or with a paste of kitchen cleanser and much rubbing. Smears of fired gold over fired color cannot be removed without using an etching solution, which also removes the color.

Liquid bright gold can be thinned, when necessary, by the addition of a drop or two of gold essence. Turpentine must never be allowed to come in contact with liquid bright gold.

Brushes used with liquid bright gold should be kept separate from painting supplies and from brushes used for burnish gold. The brushes should be cleaned in a small jar of lacquer thinner, then in clean alcohol.

Liquid bright gold can be fired at regular china firing temperatures.

When applying gold to handles, embossed designs, etc., the shader and liner brushes are used, employing the largest brush possible for the area being covered. The brush is reloaded as often as necessary, to avoid a weak application. For the application of gold to plate rims, it is possible to use the fleshy part of the index or middle finger, as follows: Holding and turning the plate on the tips of the fingers of the left hand, the fleshy part of a finger of the right hand is rubbed into the gold on the slab, then run back and forth along the rim of the plate (see Photo 1). This method produces extremely even gold bands, which can vary in width depending upon

PHOTO 1   PHOTO 2

the placement of the finger; the more the finger comes up over the plate rim, the wider will be the band.

With the use of a banding wheel, it is possible to apply bands of gold within the rim of the piece, which is done as follows: The piece to be banded with gold is carefully centered on a high-stem banding wheel; rapidly tapping the edge of the piece as the wheel turns will quickly center it. While the fingers of the left hand smoothly turn the wheel, the brush in the right hand is lowered until only the tips of the bristles contact the china, and the brush is held in this position until the band is formed (see Photo 2). Extremely fine bands of gold can be applied with a brush called a "cut liner." This brush, which is flat and has a tapered edge, is loaded with gold by "stropping" the bristles on the glass slab containing the gold; the stropping action keeps the bristles flat and assures that the loaded brush has a fine tip.

Applying Backgrounds

SEE COLOR PLATES 8 & 9, PAGES 14 & 15

One dictionary definition of the word "background" is: "The natural, physical, or material conditions that form the setting within which something is viewed or experienced." This statement expresses what the china painter tries to do with the spaces which surround a design: create a suitable setting for the painted image.

Everything in nature exists against a background; even the stars are set against infinite depths of space. In fact, it is impossible to look at an object without seeing — even unconsciously — its setting, or background. Thus, it is extremely important to the china painter that his designs are placed within a planned environment, and not just surrounded with some "pretty colors to fill the empty spots." In addition, the background should be developed along with the design and treated as a part of the whole.

As a rule, background surrounding a china painted design portrays different degrees of depth, with details becoming less distinct as they recede from the main design. This depth is very easily demonstrated by looking at an object close at hand and, without moving the eyes, taking notice of other objects nearby and those farther away. It will be noted that the closer objects will be recognizable, but will appear blurred and lose detail. Objects farther and farther away lose even more of their recognizable shapes, until those farthest away become mere impressions. This optical phenomenon can be applied to painted designs, to make the designs relate to the space around them. Items which are intended to appear to be near the main subject, such as leaves, stems and buds, will be recognizable, but not clearly defined, while far distant items will exist only as areas of color.

The actual, physical painting of background areas may be carried out in a number of ways, and partly depends on personal preference. Some painters prefer to use vigorous brushstrokes to impart suggested texture to shadow areas and distant background; other painters strive for a smoother, more delicate background. Both types of background treatment are acceptable if they are compatible with the design. Obviously, a roughly textured background would be likely to overpower a dainty design, while a delicate background would be lost against a vigorously painted design; the background is vital to the success of the finished painting; and must be consistent with and complementary to the design.

SELECTING COLORS

Colors for backgrounds should be selected with the same care used when choosing colors for designs, since they can do so much for a painting — besides filling empty space. Background colors can create the feeling of deep, reflective quiet, reminiscent of a shadowy bower — or they can cause a painting to "zing" with all the joy and beauty of a spring day — or capture the chill of winter or the warmth of summer. In addition to creating a feeling or emotion, the colors selected for backgrounds can greatly influence the way the design appears to the viewer.

As mentioned in Chapter 6, a light color can be made to appear lighter by placing it next to, or near, a dark color; and, conversely, dark colors will appear darker when adjacent to light colors. Colors of the same general value and intensity, when placed together, seem to lose the impact either color would have by itself; this color trait can be used to advantage when it is desired to minimize a portion of a design which appears brighter than planned. The color photo given here illustrates these 3 color effects.

Perhaps one of the questions most often asked by beginning painters is what actual colors can, or should, be used for backgrounds. There can really be no definite answer to such a query, but several suggested plans for selecting background colors can be recommended. Tints and shades of the same colors used in the design are always acceptable as background colors. Complementary colors can be used for backgrounds, especially when additional "punch" is needed. Perhaps one of the most often used background color schemes is the combination of blue, green and yellow. The reason that this combination is so acceptable is that these colors are representative of: atmosphere (blue), foliage (green) and sunlight (yellow), and will be suitable with any subject matter.

Once the colors for a background have been selected, they are not haphazardly applied around the design, but placed in logical sequence. The position of the light source is established and the darkest colors placed opposite in the natural shadow areas (much too often, paintings are seen in which light seems to be coming from several directions, and shadows are situated in the most impossible places). The color in the background that represents light follows a definite path through the painting, to heighten the naturalistic effect.

Shadow flowers, leaves, buds and stems, while forming part of the design, can be considered as part of the background, and all edges of these elements are blurred, to place them in their proper perspective.

One glaring flaw in much background painting, of which most painters are guilty at one time or another, is that of allowing a leaf or stem to be the dividing line between 2 background colors. It is not uncommon to see a background color – perhaps blue – painted to a stem of the design and stop, and on the other side of the stem a completely different color. Errors of this sort are easy to avoid, if the painting is viewed at a distance from time to time while it is in progress.

Sometimes, it is possible to entirely change the "mood" of

a painting by changing background colors, on the second painting. For instance, a floral design with a yellow-blue-green background, having a light and airy appearance, can be changed to a rich, formal effect by painting over the background with rich brown, violet of iron, yellow brown and a touch of persian red. When painting over a background in this manner, traces of the original colors are allowed to show here and there, for added vibrancy.

BRUSHSTROKE APPLICATION

As large a brush as is possible should be used when painting backgrounds, not only for the pleasing effect a large brush produces, but to avoid needless, tiny brushstrokes, which serve no purpose. The brushstrokes should be pulled in all directions, to avoid any set pattern — which could result if the strokes all run in the same way. An unpainted "window" here and there in the background area adds vibrancy and a feeling of movement.

Care should be taken that colors blend together softly, so that no definite change from one to the other is apparent (see the color illustration). Such blending is accomplished by very lightly stroking of one color into the other, with an almost dry brush; blending should be practiced until even complementary colors can be brushed into each other without having them turn to "mud."

DRY DUSTING

Dry dusting is an invaluable technique, not only for deepening background colors, but often for helping to "pull together" a design which seems weak, accomplished as follows: The painting is allowed to dry (usually about 24 hours) until the colors can be touched without smudging them; for this reason, dry dusting cannot be done if a non-drying medium is used for applying the paints. Some dry powder color is ground with a palette knife, to smooth it and break up any lumps. A piece of cotton batting is then used to pick up some of this dry color and applied to the desired areas, with a rouging motion. A soft brush is then used to lightly dust off any excess color, and the piece is fired in the normal manner. Dry dusting may be repeated, if necessary, on subsequent paintings (dry dusting can also be used successfully to change the color of a fired background). More than one color can be dusted onto a piece, if a separate piece of cotton is used for each one. The powdered color, or colors, remaining from the dusting process must not be mixed back into the paint supply, but should be either discarded or wrapped with the cotton in a piece of plastic and retained for dusting other pieces of china.

GROUNDING

Another method of applying background color is grounding. Grounding is used when a background of deep, solid color is desired; since grounded areas are very intense in color, this method is usually reserved for borders, bases, etc. Grounding is the most exacting method of applying color, and must be accomplished with much care. Flaws in grounded areas cannot be repaired; therefore, if the color surface is scratched or marked before the piece is fired, all of the color must be removed and the grounding applied anew.

Grounding is carried out as follows: Grounding oil (a thick oil, especially compounded for this technique) is brushed onto the desired area, as smoothly and as evenly as possible. The area is then patted with a silk-covered ball of cotton batting, until the oil is perfectly smooth and even. The piece is allowed to dry until the oil is "tacky," which usually takes about 30 minutes or longer. Smooth, powdered color is then poured onto the area and gently smoothed out with a soft brush or piece of cotton; a layer of color is maintained between the brush and the oiled area at all times, to avoid damaging the oil film. Excess color is gently removed with a soft brush.

Masking tape is used to confine grounding oil to definite areas, and is carefully removed when the color has been applied. In order to paint part of a design into a grounded area, the color is removed from the desired location, with a paper stomp or with pencil-type eraser.

The application of the various types of backgrounds should be practiced, until each one can be accomplished with ease.

Painting Daisies

SEE COLOR PLATE 10, PAGE 16

The name "daisy" can be applied to a vast number of plants, since they are members of a family (Compositae) which comprises more than 1/10 of the world's flowers. This huge family has 900 genera and over 13,000 species, and includes zinnias, asters, dahlias, chrysanthemums and dandelions, as well as food plants, such as lettuce, endive and artichoke. The plant usually referred to, when speaking of daisies, is the Bellis perennis, the common daisy of field and garden. The finer forms of this flower are popular as summer bedding plants, and are usually white, pink or red.

The name of this flower is derived from the Anglo-Saxon words meaning "day's eye," due, no doubt, to the fact that the flowers will not open on very dull days and close when the sun goes down. Some other names for daisies are: la marguerite (France), gowan (Scotland) and bairnwort, meaning "flower beloved by children" (Yorkshire section of England). Whatever they are called, whether they are cultivated or are found by the side of the road, daisies seem to have universal appeal.

Since there are so many types of daisies, it follows that the foliage of daisy-like flowers will also be found in a wide variety of shapes and sizes. The common daisy generally has rather long, tapered leaves and serrated edges, but the same leaves are also found with smooth edges; there are even daisies with foliage resembling parsley, grass and chrysanthemum leaves. This great variety of foliage makes it possible for the china painter to use any one of several types of leaves with their daisies and still have the "right" ones for the flower portrayed.

The daisy center is made up of tightly-packed florets, usually bright yellow in color. Since these center florets expand around the edges of the center disk when the flower opens, they form a round, button shape, with a depressed middle section. The flower petals (ray florets) are quilled — somewhat tubular — where they join the center, and gradually bend back into an arc as the flower ages.

The white form of the daisy is common throughout the United States, Europe and Great Britian, and is the one described in this chapter — but how do you paint a white flower?

When painting any of the small white flowers, such as daisies, fruit blossoms, lilies of the valley, etc., the beginning china painter will find it much easier to use the wipe-out method rather than direct painting. By wiping "white" flowers from a colored background, some of the surrounding colors will be incorporated into the flowers,

to give them shape and form.

PREPARATION OF
THE CHINA

To prepare a piece of china for painting daisies, tint it with mixing yellow and pat the paint with silk-covered cotton until the color is barely discernible. Fire the china to cone 017, then lightly sand it and wipe it with an alcohol-dampened cloth or paper towel.

The lower right section of the color photo given here shows a completed design, while the remaining portions show the individual paintings.

Use the china marking pencil to sketch the design onto the prepared china, or trace it on with graphite paper. (To avoid transferring overly wide lines to the china from the graphite paper, thoroughly wipe the graphite surface of the paper with a paper towel before using it.) Using a dip pen, with a fine point, go over all of the design outlines with india ink. Allow the inked design to dry, then wipe the piece with a cloth dampened with turpentine; the turpentine will remove the pencil or graphite marks, but

it will not affect the inked lines — which will burn off in the first firing.

FIRST PAINTING

Fully load a #10 shader brush with mixing yellow, and paint an area of overlapping strokes at the upper left and middle right of the design, allowing this color to go over the flowers and leaves. Pick up some pale blue on the same brush, and apply it near the bud as well as at the upper right and middle left of the design. Allow this color to also go over the flowers, and softly blend it into the yellow so that there is no definite line between the colors. Apply overlapping strokes of black green over the remainder of the design, being sure that it is strongest near the bottom, shadow area, and softly blended into adjoining colors.

Clean the brush and condition it in oil, and use it to wipe the colors from the leaves. Then lightly paint the leaves with yellow green. Paint the buds and the calyx of the partial flower at the top of the design with the same color. Wipe out the stems with the end of the brush handle.

Clean the brush and condition it in oil, and wipe out the flower petals, as follows: Place the brush at the outer edge of a petal and in one movement draw it toward the flower center. Draw the brush the length of the same petal one or 2 more times. The ridges of color remaining will simulate the lengthwise texture which daisy petals have; do not attempt to wipe the petal perfectly clean of color. Wipe out all of the petals in this manner, then remove the color from the center area. Wash over the center area with mixing yellow.

Wipe out the petals of the half flower at the top of the design, but do not clearly define every petal, since this is a background flower.

Fire the piece to cone 017, then sand it and wipe it with an alcohol-dampened cloth.

SECOND PAINTING

Sharpen the outlines of the main flowers, by darkening the background colors around them, paying particular attention to the areas where the petals join the flower centers.

Shade the leaves with olive green and brown green,

accenting the center vein lines on the more prominent ones.

Using a mixture of yellow brown and brown green in which the yellow brown predominates, shade the end of each petal near the flower center, to give the illusion that the petals are attached to the underside of the flower center. Leave an unpainted line at each side of the petals, or wipe the color from these areas, to make the petals appear tubular where they join the centers. With the same color, lightly shadow a few petals at their outer ends to make them appear bent back.

Corner-load the brush with yellow brown, and paint a "C" stroke around one side (the side nearest the light source) of each flower center. Pick up a little brown green on the same brush, and paint a smaller "C" stroke inside of the first one, to indicate the depression in the flower center. Shade the shadow side of each flower center with persian red.

Darken one side of each bud with brown green, and define the stems with the same color.

Fire the piece to cone 017, then sand it and wipe it with an alcohol-dampened cloth.

THIRD PAINTING

For this third painting, do not completely cover any area with color, but strive to heighten the realistic 3-dimensional look by carefully placing color accents.

Use a liner brush and black green to paint tiny "spaces" between the daisy petals where they join the flower center. Accent the stems with broken lines of the same color. Deepen the background areas, seen between the flower petals in the shadow areas, and the "corners" formed between the leaves.

To prevent all of the flowers from appearing to be on the same plane, wash over parts of them with background color to make them recede.

Deepen the color on the leaves in the shadow areas, using brown green and black green.

Fire the piece to cone 017.

Firing
Your China

Learning to paint china is similar to learning how to play a musical instrument — a certain amount of time must be devoted to things other than the actual painting or playing. In music, this time may be spent in learning to read music, the study of harmony and endless hours of practice; in china painting, time must be given to mixing paints, sketching from nature (hopefully), planning designs and firing the painted pieces. In china painting these extraneous endeavors often seem to require time which one would rather spend on painting, but they are all necessary to the successful completion of each project.

While most chapters in this book are devoted to the instructions for painting various designs, they are interspersed with material which is unrelated to the actual painting process, but which is, nevertheless, important; one of these subjects is firing.

Until a piece of painted china has been fired (subjected to controlled heat) in a special oven, called a "kiln," it cannot be considered complete; it must be fired, to mature the mineral colors and bond them to the glaze of the china.

Beginning china painters generally have their painted china fired by their teachers, or at a local studio, but even-

TEMPERATURE EQUIVALENTS OF
MOST COMMON PYROMETRIC CONES

CONE NUMBER	TEMPERATURE EQUIVALENT	COLOR OF KILN INTERIOR	TYPE (MATERI
6	2232° F		**Low fire porcelai and stoneware bodi(**
5	2185° F		
4	2167° F		
3	2134° F		
2	2124° F		
1	2109° F		
01	2079° F		
02	2048° F	Yellow	
03	2014° F		
04	1940° F		
05	1915° F		**Low fire cerami bodies and glaze(**
06	1830°·F		
07	1803° F		
08	1751° F	Orange	
09	1693° F		
010	1641° F		
011	1641° F		
012	1623° F		
013	1566° F	Cherry Red	
014	1540° F		
015	1479° F		**Glass saggin**
016	1458° F		
017	1377° F		**Overglaze colors, ename and ceramic deca**
018	1323° F		
019	1261° F		
020	1175° F	Dull Red	
021	1137° F		**Lustr(**
022	1112° F		

tually most will acquire a kiln of their own. The initial cost of owning a kiln is more than offset by the convenience and pleasure it affords, and the experience gained in firing a kiln is invaluable.

With the advent of light-weight refractories, shortly after World War II, small, reasonably priced electric kilns were made available to hobbyists in the fields of ceramics, enameling, glass decorating and china painting. Prior to the introduction of these kilns, the only types of kilns at the disposal of hobbyists were those fired by coal, oil or gas. Some small kilns fueled by gas or oil are in use today; but, since they are in the minority, they will not be discussed here.

Electric kilns are very reliable, safe and economical to use, and assure the user of consistent results. In addition, they are easy to operate, and can be used for years with very little, if any, need for repairs.

Electric kilns are heated by elements, which are usually made of either nichrome or kanthal wire; a third type of element is made of silicon carbide, but is seldom used in hobby kilns. Kilns with nichrome wire elements are often wired to operate from a regular household circuit, while those with kanthal elements usually require an electrical source of higher voltage.

Kilns equipped with nichrome wire elements will fire to about 1060°C, 1940°F (cone 04), which is in excess of the heat required to mature china paints, so these kilns can also be used for firing ceramics.

Kanthal elements are usually found in kilns requiring a separate 220V outlet for their operation, and are capable of bringing the kiln temperature to about 1260°C, 2300°F (cone 8); these kilns may be used for firing stoneware and porcelain, as well as for china painted pieces. If only china painting is to be fired in a kiln, one with nichrome elements will be satisfactory, and is slightly more economical to purchase and to operate. If there is any possibility that any amount of low-fire ceramic or porcelain or stoneware might be fired, a kiln equipped with kanthal elements is recommended.

SELECTING A KILN

Kilns are available in a variety of sizes, and it would be well to consider carefully before selecting one to be purchased. The natural tendency is to choose a small kiln to start with, but it should be considered that as the painter gains experience, the output of painted pieces increases, which often leads to dissatisfaction with a "too small" kiln. It should be remembered that the size of the firing chamber strictly limits the number and sizes of pieces which it can accommodate. It is far more practical, in the long run, to purchase a kiln that may at the time seem overly large, than to be disappointed later with an extremely small one. A square kiln with about a 14" or 15" square firing chamber, or a hexagonal or octagonal kiln with a firing chamber of the same dimensions, would be adequate for firing all but extremely large pieces.

All kilns are furnished with instructions and recommendations for installation and operation, and these directions should be faithfully followed. There is no more danger in firing a kiln than in operating any other piece of electrical equipment that contains heating elements — such as toasters, ovens and broilers.

It is necessary, when operating a kiln, to in some way know when a specified heat has been attained within the firing chamber; the method is the same for all ceramic processes — the use of pyrometric cones. These cones are compounded to deform at a given temperature, the number of the cone indicating the temperature at which such deformation will occur. Cones are numbered in what beginners must think to be a rather confusing method, from cone 42, which indicates a high temperature of about 3600° F, to cone 022 indicating a low temperature of 1120°F. In china painting, cones 019 (1220°F) to cone 014 (1530°) are the only ones with which the painter need be concerned, with the bulk of painted pieces being fired in the cone 018-017 range (1330 to 1420°).

Cones are used in one of two ways, for manual or automatic kiln operation. For manual operation, the cone is placed in a holder or a small pat of clay, so that it stands at an

angle of 8° from the perpendicular. Held in this manner, the cone is placed in the firing chamber of the kiln, about 3" back from a peephole, where it may be observed during the firing; when the tip of the cone bends and reaches the level of the base, the desired temperature the cone is designed to indicate has been attained and the kiln switches are turned to "off."

For automatic operation, a cone is placed in a shut-off device (optional equipment for many kilns), which automatically stops the flow of electric current when the correct temperature has been reached. The addition of an automatic shut-off to a kiln is a great convenience, and the inclusion of one is strongly recommended to anyone considering the purchase of a kiln.

Another piece of equipment to be considered is a pyrometer. A pyrometer enables the firer to be aware of the heat within the firing chamber at all times during the firing process, since it registers on a dial in 25° increments the amount of heat from 0° to 2300° (generally), or higher. A pyrometer consists of a thermocouple of two types of wire, which generate an electric current when heated; this current causes the indicator on a dial to move along a calibrated scale, or dial. A pyrometer is not intended to take the place of cones, but to indicate the rate of increase or decline of temperature within the kiln. If much firing of glass paints, or of china painted enamelware is to be done, a pyrometer is a necessity; these colors mature below the deforming temperature of cone 022.

KILN FURNITURE

The supplies called "kiln furniture" consist of shelves, posts and stilts. Shelves are made of refractory materials, and, when supported by posts, allow full advantage to be taken of the space within the firing chamber of a kiln. Several shelves of the correct size should be kept on hand. If the kiln is a large one, one or 2 half shelves may also be included, since they will allow very tall pieces to be fired along with other, smaller items without wasting space. Pieces of platten (thin boards of asbestos and clay) may also be used to increase the capacity of a kiln, by allowing large pieces to support smaller ones with the platten between them.

Posts, which are used to support the shelves, vary in height to take best advantage of kiln space. Four posts each, in a number of sizes, should be kept on hand.

Double-pointed triangular earthenware stilts are used to support and separate ware during firing, and also come in a number of sizes. A good supply of stilts in various sizes is required, and, since they break rather easily, it is best to purchase them by the dozen. Saddles, long triangular bars of the same material as stilts, will also be necessary for the firing of large, heavy pieces, such as chop plates.

STACKING THE KILN

The process of placing ware in the kiln for firing is known as "stacking," and is important for consistent, quality results. In order that the china paints become properly matured in the firing, and fire safely, some attention must be given to the stacking.

German, Japanese and French china is referred to as "hard," and pieces of china of these types may touch each other in the kiln during the firing. Most domestic china is "soft," and, consequently, must not touch other pieces during the firing because any glaze could be damaged at the point of contact. English bone china is also soft, but presents special firing problems; since it often develops "mold," or gray patches when fired, special firing directions for bone china will be covered later in this chapter. Glazed earthenware must also be handled as soft china.

Hard china plates may be fired in stacks of 4 or 5 plates, as long as stilts are placed between them; the stilts should be as large as possible for the pieces being fired, to form a sturdy stack. It is necessary to separate the pieces with stilts, to allow the heat to circulate between the pieces and evenly mature the colors on each plate. Hard china plates can also be stacked on edge, with stilts between them; it is, in fact, preferable whenever possible, to fire large plates on edge, as this position lessens the chance of cracking. Pieces stacked on edge must never touch the kiln elements, but should be supported by a fire brick or a large post propped against the side of the kiln.

There are available several different types of plate racks which can be used when firing a number of plates of the same size. These racks can be used with hard and soft china, as the holders contact only the backs of the pieces.

It is inadvisable to ever fire plates – especially large, heavy ones – directly on a kiln shelf, without the use of a stilt or saddles. The shelf, being a heavy, dense material, heats more slowly than the thinner china, and an internal stress can be set up within the china wherever it touches the cooler shelf, causing the china to crack.

China pieces other than plates – cups, bowls, vases, etc. – may also be stacked, as long as light pieces are placed upon or inside of heavier ones, with stilts separating them. Pieces of platten or a pair of saddles can be placed across the top of one piece and another piece rested on this support. Extremely tall pieces can be placed in a diagonal position, with the higher end supported by a fire brick or a large post.

It should be remembered that the stacking of pieces and the use of stilts between pieces apply only to hard china. Soft china must never touch another piece, or have a stilt placed between pieces. Each piece of soft china must be placed in a space by itself.

It should be obvious that to stack a kiln with china from the bottom to the top would invite disaster, and this is where the shelves come into play. When the bottom of a kiln has been filled with perhaps a stack of 4 or 5 plates, some cups and other smallish items, 4 posts at least 1" taller than the highest piece are evenly distributed and a shelf is rested upon them. Another group of pieces can then be stacked on the shelf, then more posts and another shelf, etc., until the kiln is full.

In the opinion of most people who fire china, a fully loaded kiln fires better than one containing only a few pieces, with a normal firing schedule. This is not to state that a person must wait until a kiln is completely filled in order to fire successfully, it is only necessary to increase the firing time when the kiln is partially filled.

FIRING

The first thing that must be considered is the temperature to which the china will be subjected, and this is, in part, a matter of personal preference. Needless to say, all colors must be fired hot enough to cause them to mature, but some china painters like to use enough heat to produce a "glaze" on their colors. It is suggested that the beginning firer try several different temperatures (by cones) to see the effects produced on the fired pieces. For the first few fires, a cone 017 is recommended.

Once the kiln has been stacked and the cone placed in position by a peephole, or in the shut-off device, the firing may begin.

The lid of the kiln should be propped open about 2", by placing under it a piece of fire brick or a post; fire brick will not conduct heat, and can be later removed with the bare hand, so it is preferred — a post will become much too hot to touch.

For kilns equipped with "on-off" switches, the bottom switch should be turned on first. For kilns with "low-medium-high" switches, the switches should be turned to low. After 1-1/2 hours, another switch is turned on, or the switches are turned to "medium." After still another 1-1/2 hours, the kiln lid should be closed and all switches turned on, or to "high." As a rule, it will then take about one more hour for the cone to bend. For manually operated kilns, it will be necessary for the firer to continually check the cone (visible through the peephole) until it bends, then all switches should be turned off. On kilns with automatic shut-off devices, the bending of the cone will trigger a switch to cut off the electric current.

The kiln should then be allowed to cool naturally, until the pieces can be removed with bare hands. It is possible to remove china from the kiln when it is still extremely hot, without damage to the pieces, but the danger of being burned and dropping the pieces makes it hardly worth the effort; unless the firer is extremely pressed for time, the kiln is allowed to cool before the china is removed.

Some colors – ruby and purple, for instance – often require a much hotter fire, while the iron red colors will fade if fired too hot. Experience is the best teacher, and firings at various temperatures will readily show the different effects on colors.

Some indications to watch for are pink colors that appear brown after firing, which means they were underfired, and the same color with a purple tone after firing, which indicates an overfire. Colors which appear very dull also indicate an underfire.

To fire partially filled kilns, the time should be extended, allowing at least 2 hours between switches.

As stated previously, English bone china is often avoided by china painters because it frequently comes from the firing covered with unsightly gray patches resembling mildew. It has been found that these blemishes almost always occur when the ware is fired too rapidly, with inadequate ventilation during the early stages of the firing. Bone china may be fired with confidence, if the firing time is extended to about six hours, and the lid of the kiln is propped open 2 or 3 inches until the interior of the kiln glows dull red (about 1000°F). This firing schedule will not adversely effect hard china, so if only one or 2 pieces of bone china are to be fired, they can be placed in the kiln with hard china, and the entire load can be fired as if it were all bone china.

KILN CARE

Modern electric kilns are designed to give years of dependable, trouble-free service, and require little care other than an occasional cleaning. The inside of the kiln should be brushed out with a soft brush, or vacuumed using the brush attachment of a vacuum cleaner. In the event that an element or switch should burn out, replacements are available from the kiln manufacturer, along with instructions for replacing the parts.

Firing a kiln will greatly increase the pleasure of china painting, and will enlarge any china painter's feeling of accomplishment.

Painting Cherries

SEE COLOR PLATE 11, PAGE 17

There are some 10 to 12 species of cherries recognized in the United States, having been carried here from Europe by the earliest settlers. Cherries are divided into 3 types – sweet, sour and dukes – the dukes being crosses of the sweet and sour types. Sweet cherry trees are rather tall, attaining heights of up to 35 feet, and produce fruit which ranges in shape from round to heart-shaped and varies in color from yellow to red to almost black. Sour cherry trees are smaller, and bear fruit which is red in color and round to oblate (flattened) in shape.

While the leaves of cherry trees vary somewhat from one species to another, they are generally long, narrow and pointed, and usually fold upward along the center vein. The leaf edges range from smooth to serrated.

The first thing to consider when painting globular shapes, such as cherries and other "round" fruit, is how light and shadow is used to create a 3-dimensional effect. Three definite areas must be included when painting rounded forms – highlight, shadow and reflected light; if the object is placed on or against something, the cast shadow must also be rendered. These variations of color represent the light, medium and dark tones of color mentioned in an earlier chapter as essential to successful 3-dimensional painting; these color tones must, of course, be relative to the overall tone of the entire composition.

Excellent practice in painting round shapes, preparatory to using cherries or other fruit as subject matter, is to draw a number of circles on a glazed tile (a quarter makes a good pattern), then apply the colors as shown in the upper left portion of the step-by-step color photos. In this exercise (see the illustrations), yellow red and blood red were the colors used. The #10 shader brush was corner-loaded with yellow red. Imagining the circle as a clock face and the light source at the upper left, the color was applied from about one to 7 o'clock. The brush was then loaded with blood red, and, with the tile turned upside down, the remaining portion of the outline was painted with a large "C" stroke. Painting the circle in this manner left an unpainted area for a highlight, at the upper left; if necessary, the edges of this highlight could be softened by tapping them with a silk-covered finger.

When all of the practice circles have been painted, the tile was fired to cone 018.

For the second painting of the circular shapes, a crescent of blood red was applied to the lower right areas, slightly within the outlines. This color is then softly blended up to the highlight area and to the lower right outlines. This blending action is necessary to soften the edges of the crescent-shaped shadow, since light flowing over a round object could not produce sharp-edged shadows.

The piece was then fired, and more color was added until the desired depth was obtained.

PREPARATION

Tint the china with mixing yellow, then fire and sand it, and wipe it with an alcohol-dampened cloth.

Use a china marking pencil to sketch the design of cherries, leaves and stems onto the prepared china, or trace it on with graphite paper.

FIRST PAINTING

Corner-load the #10 shader brush with yellow red and paint the upper left area of each cherry, beginning with those cherries which are to appear in back of others. Paint the lower right areas of the cherries with a wash of blood red, being sure to leave an unpainted highlight in the upper left area of each one. Place a piece of silk over a finger and gently tap the edges of the highlights, to soften them. Corner-load the brush with blood red, and paint a small

"C" stroke at the upper center of those cherries on which the stem depression is to show.

Paint the leaves yellow green, working from their outer edges toward the center veins. Allow the leaves to dry for a few minutes, then use a clean, oil-conditioned brush to wipe some of the color from one side of each center vein.

Lay in the branches with short, broken strokes of rich brown and black green mixed together on the brush.

Use a blunt brush handle to wipe out the cherry stems. Wipe out a small, horizontal bar at the end of each stem, within the depression in a cherry.

Fire the piece to cone 017; then sand it and wipe it with an alcohol-dampened cloth, or paper towel.

SECOND FIRE

Surround the design with background colors, using pale blue, black green and a little mixing yellow. Softly feather these colors together wherever they contact each other.

Paint a crescent shape of blood red on the lower right area of each cherry, softly blending the color off as it nears the highlight. In the same manner, blend the color toward the lower right edge of each cherry, so that a paler color tone along these edges will represent reflected light. Deepen the color in the stem depression.

Use brown green for the cherry stems and the thickened ends where they enter the depression.

Darken and model the leaves with brown green, applying the color most heavily along one side of the center veins, to make the leaves appear to fold upward.

Shade the undersides of the branches, and the shadow areas on them, with black green.

Fire the piece to cone 017; then sand it and wipe it with an alcohol-dampened cloth.

THIRD PAINTING

For this painting, do not completely cover any area with color; apply paint only where necessary to heighten the 3-dimensional effect.

Deepen the shadow areas on the cherries. Use a mixture of blood red and black green to paint the cast shadows on any cherries which are positioned in back of other cherries (remember, the light source is at the upper left, so these deep cast shadows will only be on those cherries at the right of each group).

Darken the cherry stems with a mixture of brown green and violet-of-iron. Use the same color mixture to further model the leaves, and for any shadows cast on them by cherries, branches or other leaves.

Paint the cast shadows on the branches with rich brown and black green.

Fire the piece to cone 017.

Painting Currants

SEE COLOR PLATE 12, PAGE 18

In the previous chapter, directions were given for the painting of individual round objects (cherries), and it seems only logical that the next step should be to consider the painting of groups or clusters of round fruits — a perfect example being currants.

Currants are a fruit with which many of us are familiar only in the form of jams and jellies, since they do not now enjoy the popularity they once had. Certain varieties are host for a rust which attacks several species of pine trees — valuable for lumber — and are, therefore, discouraged (or actually prohibited, in some areas). Growing on small, prickly shrubs, currants are small, juicy berries which may be red, black, or white (the white type are called "golden"). Close relatives of gooseberries (an even more prickly member of the family), currants have been cultivated for centuries in Europe and England; the European strains were transported to America by settlers of the 17th century, to be later crossed with native American varieties.

When painting clusters of fruits or berries, it is easiest in the initial painting to treat each cluster as a unit, rather than painting each element separately. This method of painting makes it simple to place the areas of light and shadow on an entire cluster at one time, rather than when each berry is individually painted; it also leaves no unpainted spaces between berries — areas which can otherwise be quite awkward to paint. The 4 color illustrations show the steps involved in using this technique.

PREPARATION

Tint the china with pale yellow brown, and pat it with a silk-covered cotton until the china appears almost white. Fire the piece to cone 017, then sand it lightly and wipe it with an alcohol-dampened cloth or paper towel.

Use the china marking pencil to sketch on the design of currants, or trace the pattern given here and then transfer it to the piece with graphite paper. If graphite paper is used, very lightly sand over the lines until they are faint but still plainly visible (sanding the graphite tracing lines will make it easier to go over them with ink). Using a dip pen, with a fine point, go over all of the design outlines with india ink. Allow the ink

to dry, then wipe the piece with a cloth dampened with turpentine; the turpentine will remove the pencil or graphite marks, but will leave the inked lines — which will disappear during the first firing.

FIRST PAINTING

Load a #6 shader brush with yellow red, and paint down the left side of the main cluster, following the outside contour. Draw this color toward the center of the cluster, cross-hatching the brushstrokes. Do the same thing to the smaller cluster at the lower right in the design, then paint the left sides of the few separate berries not included in the clusters. Load the brush with blood red and, in the same manner, paint the right sides of the clusters, drawing the color in toward their centers. Paint the left sides of the individual berries with yellow red. At this point, the piece should resemble the tile in the upper left corner of the color photo.

Use the #10 shader brush to lay in the leaves, with yellow green and warm brown green. Paint the stems·with a mixture of rich brown and black green.

Surround the design with a background of pale blue, black green and mixing yellow, blending these colors together where they meet, so that there are no definite edges to any color area. Place the darkest color (black green) up under the right sides of the clusters.

Clean the #6 shader, then dip it in tinting oil and press out most of the oil on a clean cloth. With the brush conditioned in this manner, and refreshing the condition as often as is necessary, wipe out a large highlight in the upper left of each berry in the clusters. Wipe a smaller area from the lower right side of each berry; the wiped-out areas on the lower right will serve as reflected light, and will also give the effect of transparency which juicy fruits often have. With a piece of silk placed over an index finger, wipe a sharp highlight in the upper left area of the more prominent berries.

Use a brush handle to wipe out the small berry stems.

Fire the piece to cone 017; it should then resemble the upper right section of the color photo. Lightly sand the china, then wipe it with an alcohol-dampened cloth.

SECOND PAINTING

Deepen the background colors, paying particular attention to the shadow areas under the clusters of fruit.

Corner-load the #6 shader brush with blood red, and paint a crescent shape on the lower right side of each berry; be careful that this color does not cover the reflected light. Use the same color with a touch of black green, mixed together on the brush, to deepen the color in the spaces between berries, and in the shadow area seen on the berries under the large leaf at the top of the design.

Model the leaves with olive green and brown green, darkening the color along one side of the main veins to make the leaves appear to fold along these lines.

Deepen the color on the main branches.

Fire the piece to cone 017; then sand it and wipe it, as before.

THIRD PAINTING

For this painting, do not completely cover any area with color; simply strengthen weak areas and add any

necessary details.

Corner-load the small shader brush with blood red, and deepen the center of the shadow on each berry. Then on the same brush, pick up some blood red and black green, and paint the cast shadows on those berries which are behind others; remember that the light source (indicated by the highlights) is at the upper left, so any cast shadows would have to be to the right. Load the pointer brush with black green and black, and paint a dot of this mixture on each berry to represent the bud end. Each bud is exactly opposite the berry stem, so they must be placed near the bottoms of the berries.

Deepen the color on the leaves, lightly indicating secondary veins along the main ones. Touch the very edges of the leaves, here and there, with tiny specks of violet of iron, to simulate the serrated edges which currant leaves have.

Paint shadows of rich brown on the branches under the leaves and berries.

Fire the piece to cone 017.

The Christmas Rose and Holly

SEE COLOR PLATE 13, PAGE 19

Helleborus niger, the Christmas rose, is a plant often associated with stories of the Nativity, since it blooms in midwinter. The most prevalent legend tells of an angel scattering the beautiful white roses before a little shepherd girl who had no gifts to offer the Christ Child. Another version of the tale says that the flowers sprang up when the little girl's tears fell to the ground. Both versions of the legend claim that these never-before-seen flowers have bloomed ever since, always during the Christmas season.

The white cup-shaped "petals" of the Christmas rose are actually sepals surrounding tubular green petals, much as the red bracts of a poinsettia surround the insignificant flowers of that plant. The leaves of the Christmas rose are dark green and divided into seven-to-nine segments; being rather large, the leaves are difficult to include in a design, so the flower pictured in the color photo is surrounded by holly — another plant closely associated with the Christmas season.

The use of holly as a Christmas decoration has its roots in antiquity, dating to the Teutonic practice of hanging evergreens indoors, to shelter the woodland spirits from the winter weather. Like the Christmas rose, many legends have been associated with holly.

There are many varieties of holly, and the trees range in size from 50' giants to shrub-like plants of only 6'. The leaves are leathery and ever-green, and the fruit is usually round and red in color —

though there are some species which produce white, yellow or black berries.

A modified version of the wipe-out method is used to paint large white flowers, which differs slightly from the technique described in Chapter 10 (Painting Daisies). This and the previously described technique can be used to paint almost any type of white flower.

PREPARATION

Tint the china with mixing yellow, brushing it on and then patting it with silk-covered cotton batting until the china once again appears white. Fire the piece to cone 017; then sand it lightly and wipe it with an alcohol-dampened cloth or paper towel.

Use the china marking pencil to sketch the design onto the prepared china, or trace it on with graphite paper. If desired, use a pen with a fine point to go over all of the design outline with india ink; allow the ink to dry, then wipe the piece with a cloth dampened with turpentine. The inking of design outlines has been mentioned in several previous chapters as an aid to

beginning painters, but may be dispensed with as the painter gains confidence and skill.

FIRST PAINTING

Fully load a #10 shader brush with black green, and paint the background around the upper 2/3 of the design. Pick up some pale blue on the same brush, and paint the remaining background areas. Use the same colors to fill in the openings between the leaves and flowers.

Wash over the leaves with yellow green, adding a touch of brown green in the shadow areas. The painting at this point should appear like the one in the upper left section of the color photo.

Apply a wash of mixing yellow to the flower center, lightly feathering the color up into the petals.

Use a tiny bit of brown green on the corner of the brush, to indicate the petal separations on the flowers and bud.

Use a small brush to paint the holly berries with yellow red on the light sides and blood red on the shadow sides. Be sure to leave a large highlight on the upper right area of

each berry, or wipe it out with a silk-covered fingernail.

Fire the piece to cone 017; then sand it and wipe it with an alcohol-dampened cloth.

SECOND PAINTING

Wash over the bud and the lower half of the large flower with pale blue; then apply a wash of black green over the upper left section of the large flower. Clean the brush, then use it to wash mixing yellow over the remainder of the large flower and all of the half flower. Allow these washes of color to "set up" for a few minutes while working on the rest of the design.

Darken the background in the corners formed by the joining of leaves and petals, paying particular attention to the openings between the design elements.

Model the leaves, using olive green, and a mixture of olive green and brown green for the shadow areas. Use a clean, conditioned brush to wipe a few veins from each leaf.

Deepen the color on the shadow side of each berry, being sure to avoid the highlight.

Clean and condition the shader brush, then use it to wipe color from the flowers and buds, to shape the petals, as follows: Use the corner of the brush to wipe the color from the turn-backs, at the ends of the petals on the large flower. Then wipe out the petal edges, leaving touches of the color washes on each petal. Pull the edge of the brush down the length of each petal, to simulate the characteristic ridge found on each petal. Wipe out the edges of the petals on the bud and half flower, in the same way.

Use a blunt brush handle to wipe out 8 or nine curved lines in the center of the open flower, for the stamens (these are really the flowers of the Christmas rose, but we will refer to them as stamens).

Fire the piece to cone 017; then sand and wipe it with alcohol.

THIRD PAINTING

Paint the stamens with light yellow brown; then use a pointed brush to place a dot of black green at the end of each one. Allow these colors to set for a few minutes; then, with a sharpened brush handle, wipe around each spot of black green and down the length of each stamen.

Corner-load the shader brush with rich brown, and paint sharp tips on the points of the leaves.

Use a pointed brush and a mixture of black green and black to paint the bud ends on the berries.

Fire the piece to cone 017.

Painting Roses

PART I

SEE COLOR PLATE 14, PAGE 21

Roses are without a doubt the world's most popular flowers, and must be judged as especially admired by china painters, according to the frequency of their use as subject matter. Countless pieces of china have been decorated with rose designs since the advent of overglaze colors; yet paintings of these beautiful blossoms never seem to lose their appeal.

Native to the Northern Hemisphere, roses have adorned this section of the globe for literally millions of years; fossil remains of roses discovered in Colorado are believed to be at least thirty-five million years old. Pictures of roses have been discovered which date back to the 16th century B.C., and the island of Rhodes, which takes its name from the rose, had them engraved on coins as early as 4000 B.C. Honored by the ancient Romans and Greeks, roses played an important part in many of their ceremonies, being worn by the participants, while rose petals were lavishly strewn on the floors and furnishings of homes and temples.

The term "sub rosa" (under the rose), indicating something that is private or confidential, comes from the ancient custom of hanging a rose under which all present were sworn to secrecy. This custom, no doubt, derives from the legend of Cupid giving a rose to Harpocrates, the god of silence, to keep him from telling the love affairs of Venus.

Roses have also played a part in religion, often associated with the Virgin Mary. In fact, the rosary was named for a wreath given to St. Dominick by the Virgin, and early rosaries were actually composed by beads made from tightly pressed rose petals.

This and several subsequent chapters will be devoted to the painting of roses, so that descriptions may be given of painting the flowers in various stages of development and as they would be viewed from several different angles. This first part will consider a rose in full bloom, at what is called a 3/4 angle.

To illustrate how a rose can be drawn when comparing it to familiar objects, a cup and saucer are used to represent the general shape of the flower. Figure 1 shows a cup and saucer, with the opening of the cup representing the heart, or opening in a rose; the sides of the cup depicting the bowl, or petals which surround the heart; and the

saucer indicating turned-back petals, around the bowl. Each part of this diagram comprises about 1/3 of the total height of the drawing.

Figure 2 indicates how a light source at the upper left would cause shadows within and on the cup and saucer. Light would affect a rose in the same way: the deepest shadow within the heart would be toward the light, and the side of the bowl furthest from the light would be shadowed and cast a shadow on the turned-back petals. In addition, reflected light (light bouncing back from the lower petals) would cause a lighter shadow area along the edge of the bowl.

Figure 3 shows the outline of a rose superimposed on the cup and saucer outline, to illustrate how the various parts – heart, bowl and petals – fit within the general cup and saucer shape. To avoid a completely oval shape, which would result if the entire rose were kept within the cup and saucer outline, one or 2 petals are allowed to extend beyond the outline.

Figure 4 shows how petals are added within the outlines,

to complete the drawing of the rose. (A future chapter will describe in more detail the drawing of roses and placement of the petals.)

Many beginning china painters, for one reason or another, find it necessary to work without the benefit of a teacher; therefore, while the following directions may seem somewhat unorthodox, they are designed to aid the self-taught painter. This method of painting is intended only as an introduction to painting roses, and to serve as a "crutch" which may be discarded when the technique has been mastered.

One difference in this method and others that have been covered is the tinting of the china. Previous directions have called for the china to be tinted with one or more colors which are padded to a smooth, almost colorless ground; for roses, the tinting is done so that definite areas receive a tint of specific color.

FIRST PAINTING

Trace the outlines on Figure 5 onto a piece of thin paper, then transfer them to the china with graphite paper. The large outlined area represents the rose and the smaller areas

represent the leaves.

Load a #10 shader brush with pale pink, and fill in the rose shape with large, loose strokes. Pick up some dark pink and lightly paint in shadows as indicated in Figure 2, as follows: Assuming the rose is the face of a clock with the top center being 12 o'clock, start on the turned-back petals at 9 o'clock and draw the brush down along the contour of the bowl to 6 o'clock. Now turn the piece upside-down and paint several strokes of dark pink on the bowl. Turn the piece right-side-up, and, starting at the left side of the heart, fill this area with overlapping comma strokes of dark pink; the darkest color will be deposited at the left of the heart and gradually lighten as the color is exhausted while moving toward the right side of the heart.

Clean the brush; then condition it in tinting oil and press it on the painting cloth, to remove the excess oil. With the clean, oiled brush, wipe a large highlight from the left side of the bowl.

Clean the brush, then load it with yellow green. Paint loose, occasionally overlapping

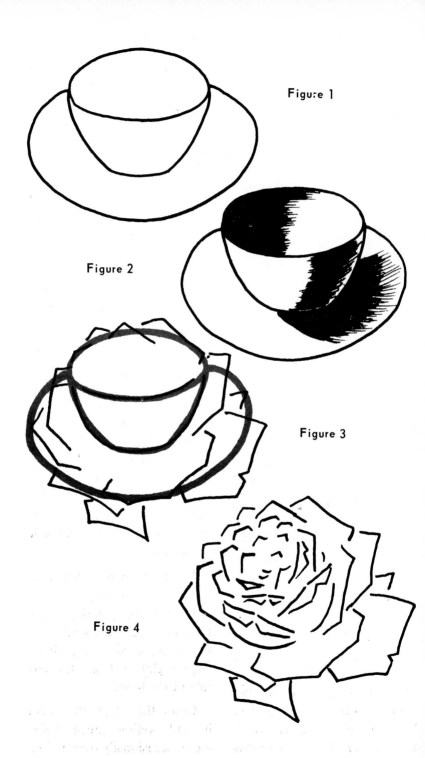

Figure 1

Figure 2

Figure 3

Figure 4

strokes of this color over the leaf areas, being sure to allow the color to extend beyond the outlines.

Fill in the remaining areas around the rose and leaf colors with black green, pale blue and yellow, lightly brushing these colors into each other where they join, to avoid hard lines between them.

Clean the brush and condition it with oil; then lightly brush over the edges of the rose area, to blur the outlines.

The upper left section of the color photo shows the painting at this stage, with the outlines clearly visible.

Fire the piece to cone 017, lightly sand it, then wipe it with an alcohol-dampened cloth. (The upper right portion of the photo shows the piece after this first firing.)

SECOND FIRING

Trace the drawing in Figure 6 onto a piece of light paper.

Position the tracing on the piece so that the outlines of the rose match the fired pink color. Holding the tracing in this position, slip a piece of graphite paper under it and trace over all of the lines, to transfer them to the china. Very lightly sandpaper the piece, until the graphite lines appear faint but still visible.

Using a dip pen with a fine point, go over all of the lines with india ink. Allow the ink to dry; then wipe the piece with a turpentine-dampened cloth, to remove any remaining graphite (the turpentine will not affect the india ink, which will disappear when the piece is later fired).

Use the #10 brush to apply a fairly heavy coat of pink to the light areas of the rose, then cover the dark shadow areas with dark pink. Allow these colors to dry for a few minutes while painting the leaves and stems.

Load the #6 brush with brown green and a little olive green. Paint each leaf from the outer edges toward the center vein. Clean the brush and condition it in oil, then press it against the paint cloth to remove the excess oil. Now use the brush to wipe a highlight from one side of each leaf, and the corner of the brush to wipe out a few small side veins. Paint the stems with the leaf colors, adding a touch of violet of iron.

Darken the background around the rose, paying particular attention to the "corners" formed by overlapping petals.

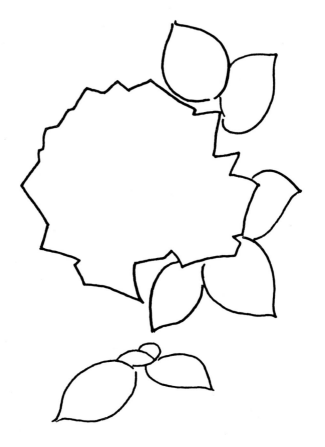

Figure 5

Clean and condition the #10 brush and use it to wipe out petals in the rose, as follows: once again thinking of the rose as a clock face, start at 11 o'clock and work counter clockwise, "cutting" and "pulling" highlights on each outer petal.

The term "cut" means to pull the knife edge of the brush sideways, so that a line is wiped from the paint; to "pull" means to place the full width of the brush and move the brush as though applying color. In wiping out petals as directed above, a cut (line) is made along each outline of each outer petal, then the brush is placed on the line and pulled back toward the center of the flower. This action will result in petals which appear to roll under softly, as the outer petals on a rose actually do.

Now, use the same brush to cut the upper edges of the petals which cross the bowl, then "push" the paint back from the cut lines. When paint is to be "pushed," the full width of the brush is placed on the china, and is then pushed away with an almost scooping motion. This movement causes a fine line of paint to be pushed ahead of the brush and deposited when the brush is lifted from the china. In making rose petals, it results in petals which appear to fold and project toward the viewer.

Indicate the small petals which appear in the heart of the rose, by pushing the paint upward with the corner of the brush.

Allow the piece to dry, then fire it to cone 017. Lightly sand the china, and wipe it with an alcohol-dampened cloth.

THIRD PAINTING

Do not completely cover any area with color, but add necessary accents, shadows and details.

Mix together on the shader brush some dark pink and a little black green. Apply this color in the deep shadow areas on the right side of the rose.

Add shadows to the leaves, with a mixture of brown green and violet of iron. Use the same colors for the shadow areas of the stems. Paint tiny touches of violet of iron along a few of the leaf edges, to represent the serrated edges which real rose leaves have.

Fire the piece to cone 017. If any difficulty should be

Figure 6

encountered in wiping out the rose petals for the second firing, the paint may be wiped off with turpentine, as often as is necessary, without damaging the inked lines.

Painting Roses

PART 2

SEE COLOR PLATES 15 & 16, PAGES 22 & 23

It is desirable, when painting any flower, to portray it in different stages of development; this is especially true of roses, which change dramatically in shape as they grow from bud to full bloom to fully open flowers. PART I of this chapter contains directions for painting a rose at the peak of bloom, with only a few petals folded back, while the remaining petals retain something of the bud shape. As the rose blossom develops, the petals fold back, layer by layer, until the center containing the stigma and stamens is exposed. The flowers are lovely when they are open to this extent, and paintings of them add greatly to any rose design.

The folding back of the rose petals changes the entire contour of the flower, from the cup and saucer shape (mentioned in PART 1), to an outline more similar to a sauce dish and saucer. Figure 1 shows such a shape, and how light (in this case, coming from the upper left) would affect the shadow areas. The saucer shape still represents the first row of turned-back petals, while the sauce dish represents the remaining ones; the bottom of the sauce dish represents the area comprised of the stigma and stamens. It should be noted that the right side of the diagram remains in deep shadow, but the shadow area on the inside of the dish is quite small — due to the open and therefore large, fairly flat shape.

Figure 2 illustrates how the fully open rose takes the saucer and sauce dish shape, with one or 2 petals extending beyond the outline, to avoid having the flower completely contained within the oval.

The procedure for painting a rose described in **PART 1** will be used to paint a fully opened rose, but it should be remembered that this method is intended only as an aid in learning the placement of petals. Once the method of cutting petals has been learned, the tracing of the petal outlines should be discarded; with practice, the china painter will be able to place petals by "eye," resulting in painted designs which are softer and more natural in appearance.

FIRST PAINTING

Trace the outlines of the flower and leaves in Figure 3 onto a piece of thin paper, then transfer them to the china with graphite paper.

Pick up a small amount of pompadour on a #10 shader brush, then work the brush hairs back and forth on a clean space on the palette until the brush contains only a light tint of the color. Wash over all of the petal shapes below the bowl line, and the tips of the petals along the upper edge of the flower. Pick up a little more pompadour, and apply it

to the shadow area on the lower left side and one or 2 brushstrokes at the upper right; these darker areas correspond to the cast shadows indicated in Figure 1.

Clean the brush, then pick up some mixing yellow and apply it to the center area of the flower. Lightly feather this color into the pompadour along the upper edge.

Wash over the leaf shapes with chartreuse, allowing the color to extend beyond the outlines.

Fill the remaining areas with the background colors of black green, pale blue and yellow. Softly brush these colors into one another where they join, until there are no definite lines between them.

Clean the brush and condition it in oil. Lightly brush over the edges of the rose area with the conditioned brush, to blur the outlines. The upper left area of the step-by-step color photo shows the painting at this stage.

Fire the piece to cone 017; then lightly sand it, and wipe it with an alcohol-dampened cloth.

SECOND PAINTING

Trace the drawing in Figure

FIGURE 1

FIGURE 2

153

4 onto a piece of light paper. Position the tracing on the china so that the outlines of the rose are directly over the fired pompadour area. Slip a piece of graphite paper under the tracing, then go over all of the lines to transfer them to the china. Very lightly sandpaper the piece, until the graphite lines become very faint but still visible. Using india ink and a dip pen and a fine point, go over all of the lines. Allow the ink to dry; then wipe the piece with a cloth dampened with turpentine, to remove the remaining graphite (the turpentine will not affect the india ink, which will disappear when the piece is fired). The upper right section of the step-by-step color photo shows the ink tracing over the fired color.

Apply a light coat of pompadour to the lower part of the flower and to the edges of the upper petals. Apply a deeper tone of the same color to the shadow areas. Paint the stigma in the center of the rose with olive green; then wash over the remaining unpainted portion of the flower with mixing yellow and light yellow brown. Allow these colors to "set" for a few minutes, while you paint the leaves and stems.

Load the #6 brush with brown green and a little olive green. Apply this color mixture to each leaf, working from the outer edges toward the center vein. Clean the brush, condition it in oil, press it on the paint cloth to remove the excess, and use it to wipe a highlight from one side of each leaf; also wipe out a few small side veins, with the corner of the same brush. Paint the stems with a mixture of brown green and violet of iron.

Deepen the background colors, being sure to apply rich color to the corners formed by overlapping petals and leaves. Then use a clean, conditioned brush to gently pull a little of the background colors over the edges of the rose.

Starting at the upper left side of the flower, use the clean, conditioned, #10 brush to cut and pull highlights on each of the outer petals (see PART 1 of this chapter for the definition of "cutting" and "pulling").

Use the corner of the same brush to wipe out the petals which cross the front of the rose. Place the full width of the brush on these wiped-out

FIGURE 3

FIGURE 4

petal lines and PUSH the brush toward the bottom of the flower.

Make the tips of the petals along the upper edge of the rose by PUSHING the paint upward with the corner of the brush.

Load the tip of a liner brush with dark yellow brown, and make many, tiny dots around the edge of the green stigma; these dots will represent the ends of the stamens, and should extend outward from the stigma into the heart of the flower, in an uneven manner. Allow the yellow brown color to dry for a few minutes; then use a brush handle or a wooden skewer to knock out tiny open areas in the yellow brown dots, to give the stamens a soft, fluffy appearance.

Allow the piece to dry; then fire it to cone 017. Lightly sand the china, and wipe it with an alcohol-dampened cloth.

THIRD PAINTING

Strengthen any weak areas of color on this painting, but do not completely cover any area with color.

Corner-load a shader brush with a little violet of iron, and paint the edges of a few of the leaves; use the same color for the shadow areas on the stems. Add a few tiny dots of rich brown in the shadow areas of the stamens.

Fire the piece to cone 017.

Now, take the bull by the horns and, using the information from this chapter, paint a design combining the full rose and the fully open rose; the full-page color study illustrates such a design. Sketch the design freehanded, if possible, or trace just the basic flower shapes and cut out the petals without the use of inked lines — only by such practice will the painting of roses become spontaneous and result in truly original finished pieces.

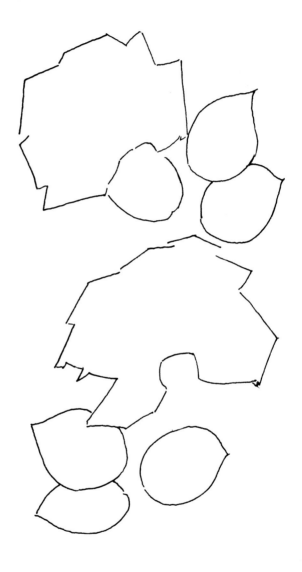

FIGURE 1

CHAPTER 15 — PART 3

Painting Roses

PART 3

SEE COLOR PLATES 17 & 18, PAGES 24 & 25

Side and back views of roses can add interest to paintings, when used as parts of the main design; blossoms in these positions can also be used effectively as shadowy flowers, to fill in vacant areas.

When a rose is viewed from the side, the ovary and the calyx are exposed, and these, too, can add interest to a design. There are 5 leaf-like sepals which form the calyx; these sepals enclose the bud and, as the flower opens, they fold back to surround the ovary and lie along the stem. The outsides of the sepals are the same color as the leaves of the plant; the insides of them, which are visible when they fold back, are a pale, cool green and, with age, become red brown along their edges.

The ovary is the seed-bearing part of the flower, and becomes larger as the flower matures and seeds develop within it. When the flower loses its petals and the sepals finally dry up, the round, fleshy pod is called a rose hip, or rose haw.

The shape of a rose when it is turned over is very much like the back of a sauce dish, the foot of the dish corresponding to the point at which the petals join the calyx. The entire flower would be contained within the oval outline of the dish. Only the outside petals are completely visible in this position, with the edges of the inner petals showing between and above these outside petals.

The same method is used to paint the side view of a rose as described in PARTS 1 and 2 of this chapter; but, once again, it is stressed that tracings of the separate petals should be used only for practice, until the petals may be placed freely without tracings.

FIRST PAINTING

Trace the outlines of the drawing in Figure 1, and transfer them to the china with graphite paper.

Use a #10 square shader brush to apply a light coat of mixing yellow to the roses. Then pick up some pale yellow brown and apply it to the shadow area of each flower; the shadow areas will be on the lower right of each rose.

Clean the brush and condition it in oil, and use it to wipe a highlight from the left side of each rose.

Wash over the leaf shapes with chartreuse, allowing the color to extend beyond their outlines.

Surround the rose and leaf shapes with background colors of black green, pale blue and a little pale violet. Be sure to softly brush these colors into each other where they join, to avoid having definite lines between them.

Clean the brush and condition it in oil, then use it to gently brush over the edges of the roses, to break up any definite outlines. (This stage of the painting is illustrated by the upper left section of the step-by-step color photo.)

Fire the piece to cone 017. Lightly sand the painted surface of the piece, then wipe it with an alcohol-dampened cloth.

SECOND PAINTING

Trace all of the outlines in Figure 2 onto a piece of light paper. Position this tracing on the china so that the outlines of the roses are directly over the fired mixing yellow areas. Slip a piece of graphite paper under the tracing, then trace over the pattern outlines to transfer them to the china. Lightly sandpaper the piece, until the graphite lines are faint but still visible. Using a pen with a fine point, go over all of the lines with india ink. Allow the ink to dry, then use a cloth dampened with turpentine to remove all traces of graphite from the surface of the piece. (The upper right section of the step-by-step color photo shows the ink tracing over the fired color.)

Apply a light coat of mixing yellow to the left side of each flower. Pick up some yellow brown on the same brush and apply it to the right sides of the flowers. Allow these colors to set for a few minutes, while painting the leaves and stems; it is much easier to cut petals from paint which has been allowed to stand until some of the oil has evaporated.

Load a #6 shader brush with brown green, and use it to shade the leaves. Pick up some violet-of-iron on the same brush and paint the ends of the sepals and all of the stems.

Deepen the background colors around the design, being sure that the colors are rich in the shadow areas and in the corners formed between petals and leaves. Gently pull a little of the background colors over the edges of the roses.

Use a clean, conditioned brush to wipe most of the color from the center sepal of the upper flower, and from the left sepal of the lower one. Then "cut" the petals which cross the flowers, and push the paint away from these cut lines toward the bottoms of the flowers.

To make the calyxes look as though they are tucked up under the flower petals, use the conditioned brush to wipe the petal color from across the calyxes.

Allow the piece to dry; then fire it to cone 017. Lightly sand the china, then wipe it with an alcohol-dampened cloth. (The painting at this stage is illustrated by the lower left area of the step-by-step color photo.)

THIRD PAINTING

Corner-load a shader brush with just a touch of yellow brown, and use it to accent the turned-back petals of the roses. Strengthen any weak areas, but do not completely cover any area with color. Add a little violet-of-iron to the edges of one or 2 leaves and to the edges of the sepals.

Fire the piece to cone 017. Now, try painting an

arrangement of roses, using the information from all parts of this chapter. Practice cutting out petals without the aid of inked lines. The rose design in the large color illustration was painted as described above, but in the second painting rich brown, dark yellow brown and violet-of-iron were pulled over the background colors, for an entirely different finished effect.

FIGURE 2

Painting Roses

PART 4

SEE COLOR PLATES 19 & 20, PAGES 26 & 27

It is often desirable, when painting roses, to include in the design buds in their several stages of development; in fact, buds by themselves can be successfully worked into designs which are for borders and other small areas. The full-page color photo illustrates how buds of various types can be incorporated into a design.

The shape of a newly formed bud is interesting, since it allows the urn-like hypanthium, often called the "hip," to be seen. This fleshy receptacle at the base of the bud will, as the flower matures, produce seeds. The petals of the bud are encased by 5 separate sepals, which, as they unfold, form the characteristic rose calyx. Sepals are leaf-like in shape, and tightly overlap each other in the newly formed bud. As the bud matures, the sepals fold back to reveal the tightly furled petals, and eventually curl back along the stem, often hiding the hip from view. The inside surface of the sepals — the side which shows when folded back — is generally lighter in color than the outside, becoming (with age) a red-brown color, similar to violet-of-iron china paint.

During the maturing process, the petals within the sepals begin to grow and swell, causing the sepals to separate and allow the color of the petals to be seen. Later, as the sepals begin to fold back toward the stem, they reveal the tightly furled petals, which then begin to unfold into a fully developed flower.

The 4 color photos illustrate the painting of rose buds in these various stages.

CLOSED BUD

To paint a closed bud, use a small (#4), pointed shader quill brush. Load the brush with brown green, and, with the china turned so that the tip of the proposed bud will be facing toward yourself, paint a line for the stem. As the brush nears the bud end of the stem, swing it in a half circle to the left, to form one side of the hip; then use slightly more pressure on the brush at this point, to cause it to fan out, filling the shape with shaded color (see Fig. 1, in the step-by-step color photo). Place the brush at the end of this just completed stroke, and pull the brush as if you were going to write the top half of the letter "S," gradually diminishing the pressure on the brush, to form a point at the tip of the bud (see Fig. 2). Pick up a little antique green on one side of the brush, and paint another stroke of the same shape inside of the previous one; this will form the edge of another sepal (see Fig. 3). This completes one half of the bud.

Turn the china so that the stem end of the bud is toward yourself, and complete the bud, as follows: Place the brush at the tip of the bud and pull down toward the base, swinging out in a bowl shape and back in to join the strokes on the first half of the bud (see Fig. 4). Complete the bud shape by forming the remaining half of the hip and the stem (see Fig. 5). Clean the brush and condition it in oil then wipe out the left side of the center sepal (see Fig. 6).

For buds which are warmer in color tone, use brown green for the shadow side and yellow green for the highlight side. Shadow buds can be painted with Copenhagen gray, or gray tones made by mixing complementary colors; for more elusive looking, "shadow" buds wash over them with background colors on subsequent paintings.

PARTIALLY OPEN BUDS

Buds which have begun to swell so that the petal color is visible between the separating sepals are painted as are closed buds, except that the sepals are painted over a patch of the rose color, as follows:

Load the pointed shader brush with the color of the rose in the design (pompadour was used for the color illustration) and paint an oval (see Fig. 7). Then, following the directions for the closed bud, pull the sepal color over the patch of petal

color. Deepen the petal color, if necessary, on subsequent paintings.

By painting over the petal color as described above, the sepals will actually seem to enfold the petals – an effect which cannot be achieved by painting the petal color between the sepals.

OPENING BUDS

When the sepals surrounding a rose bud begin to fold back, the entire bud is exposed and petal by petal starts to unfurl. To paint such a bud, use a square shader brush to wash in the bud shape with the rose color, being sure to shadow one side and highlight the other (see Fig. 7). Then use the pointed brush to paint the stem and hip with brown green. Paint the sepals by placing the pointed brush at the spot where the bud and hip join, then apply pressure to the brush as it is pulled away from the bud and gradually decrease this pressure, to form the point of the sepal (see Fig. 8). Clean the pointed brush and condition it in oil, then use it to wipe the color from the broad end of each sepal (see Fig. 9); this will make the sepals appear to stand out from the bud.

Fire the piece to cone 017;

then sand it and wipe it with a alcohol-dampened cloth.

Load the square shader brush with the rose color and wash over the bud; then apply darker tone of color on the shadow side. Corner-load the brush with rose color, and pain a small triangular shape at the tip of the bud, to represent the opening. Clean and condition the brush, and use it to cut petal from the tip of the bud to its base (see Fig. 10). Corner-load the brush with brown green, and shade the hip directly under the sepals. Pick up a little violet of iron on the same brush and apply it to the tips of the sepals.

FULLY OPEN BUDS

A fully open bud is very much like a rose in full bloom and is painted in the same manner – the difference between the bud and the rose being the overall shape. A fully open bud retains something of the elongated outline of the closed bud; the bowl is deep and broad at the bottom and the heart is higher and narrower than that of the full rose.

The lower left section of the step-by-step color photo shows the similarity in painting this type of bud and painting a full rose.

Painting Roses

PART 5

SEE COLOR PLATES 21 & 22, PAGES 28 & 29

Foliage plays an important part in the successful painting of roses (as it does in any floral or fruit painting), and much time and practice should be devoted to the correct portrayal of leaves and stems. Special attention should also be directed to depicting the proper leaf for the flower being painted; it is all too common to see china painted pieces with roses, pansies, grapes, etc., etc., etc., all with leaves of exactly the same shape. Mother Nature, the most consummate artist, has designed a unique leaf for each of her creations, and those of us who attempt to capture these superlative bits of nature

with brush and paint should strive to do so as accurately as possible. Even though the style a painter develops may be somewhat impressionistic, a lily leaf still does not grow on a rose bush!

The most perfect way to study foliage is, of course, to collect actual leaf samples and preserve them for future use; this, in itself, affords a good deal of pleasure and satisfaction. There are any number of ways to preserve and display leaves, but one which takes little time and material, and provides an ideal source of reference material for the china painter, is as follows: Fresh, well-formed leaves are picked and dried in a commercial flower-drying compound, or in equal parts of white corn meal and borax powder. The dry leaves are then arranged on the sticky side of a piece of colorless, transparent contact paper and covered with another piece of the same material. This leaf "sandwich," which is quite durable, is then cut to the size of a loose-leaf binder page, punched and stored in a notebook. As long as the leaves are thoroughly dry when they are laminated between the sheets of contact paper, they last almost indefinitely. To make this collection even more complete, a small slip of paper showing the type of leaf and other pertinent data can be laminated along with each leaf or group of leaves.

In addition to the collection of actual leaves, there are countless sources of readily-available material with color photos or accurate paintings, such as seed and plant catalogs, nature books and textbooks. Any or all of these materials will be of interest to the serious painter.

Leaves are classified by their shapes and margins; each rose leaf being referred to as simple, oval and serrate (sharp-toothed), arranged in a pinnate (matching on either side of a stalk) fashion in groups of 3, 5 or 7, the end leaf being larger than the others. The groups of leaves are arranged alternately on a stem and often have a leaf-like stipule growing at the base of the leaf stalk. Rose leaves (and many other types of leaves) fold slightly upward along the center vein, each half of the leaf being somewhat convex in shape.

PAINTING LEAVES

There are various methods of painting leaves, and each painter eventually settles on one which suits his particular style. The procedure described below is very basic and is easily learned.

Assuming that the design has been sketched or traced onto the china, paint the leaves, as follows:

FIRST FIRE

Load a shader brush with chartreuse, and, starting at the outer edge of the leaf, draw the brush toward the center vein (see Fig. 1 in the drawings.) Repeat this step, overlapping succeeding strokes until about 3/4 of this side of the leaf is filled with color (see Fig. 2). Then, placing the brush on the vein line on the unpainted half of the leaf, paint overlapping strokes to fill in about 3/4 of this area (see Fig. 3). Turn the china so that the tip of the leaf is toward yourself, and place the brush so that it is across the center vein line at about a 45° angle; pull downward, making a diamond-shaped stroke, to fill in the leaf tip. Repeat this process for each leaf in the group, painting each one as though the entire leaf were visible. Allow the paint to set up for a few moments, then use a clean, oil-conditioned brush to wipe the color from some areas of the foremost leaves; this action will make these leaves appear to be on top of others in the group. The upper left portion of the color photo illustrates this step.

Fire the china, then lightly sand it and wipe it with an alcohol-dampened cloth.

SECOND FIRE

Load the shader brush with a mixture of brown green and olive green, and paint along the outer edges of the leaves, but do not draw the brush all the way to the center vein. Then make several strokes toward the center at an angle, to indicate the side veins. Corner-load the brush with brown green, and deepen the color on the leaf tips. Use a silk over a finger to wipe sharp highlights from the edge of any leaf where it overlaps another, to heighten the naturalistic effect.

Leaves painted as described above may be used in a design, but if all leaves were to be painted in the same position, the finished design would appear flat and artificial. To avoid this "corsage" look, learn to think of and paint leaves in some ways other than "head-on" positions. The upper right section of the color photo shows the same 5 leaves, but this time they were arranged as if the entire group had been turned to lie flatly at eye level. Learning to paint leaves in various positions will be simplified if real leaves or paper cut-outs of leaf shapes are held before the eyes and gradually turned and twisted with the fingers; for instance,

an oval rose leaf will appear as a heart shape when held at eye level with the tip toward the viewer. Practice making pencil sketches of these hand-held leaves, then translate the sketches into paintings; the groups of leaves in the lower sections of the color photo are the result of such practice. Whenever possible, observe and sketch leaves as they grow on a living plant, keeping a sketched record — as suggested in Chapter 7, and illustrated here by the black and white photo.

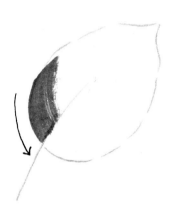

FIG. 1   FIG. 2

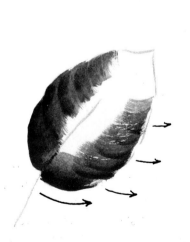

FIG. 3   FIG. 4

ROSE LEAVES

STEMS

Rose stems are generally smooth, punctuated along their lengths with sharp, downward-slanting thorns. The stems do not, as a rule, grow straight from base to blossom, but change directions slightly at each leaf stalk junction. In varieties of roses which have clusters of buds and blossoms, the bud stems angle sharply away from the main stalk. The stems vary in color, from the fresh bright green of new growth to the red-green color of more mature branches.

A simple but effective way to paint stems is with a corner-loaded shader brush, as follows: Corner-load a brush with warm brown green (for new growth), or warm brown green and a little violet-of-iron (for older stock). With the corner of the brush towards the outer edge of one side of the stem, sweep along its length with short, broken strokes. Turn the china and paint the other side in the same manner. This will result in stems which appear round, having a highlight along their length.

To add thorns to the stems, corner-load the brush with violet-of-iron, and, starting at the edge of the stem, pull downward and away, then back to slightly below the starting point. The direction of the brush movements in painting thorns is illustrated in the lower right portion of the color photo.

DEWDROPS

It is sometimes desirable to add interest to flower and fruit paintings by including related details, dewdrops being one of the most often used. To paint a dewdrop, wipe out the shape before the china is fired, when the first painting is otherwise completed. On the second painting, shade the dewdrop on the side toward the light source, using the color of the leaf or petal on which it is resting, being sure to leave strong highlights along the shadow side and along the bottom; highlights in a dewdrop should be completely free of color. Paint a cast shadow on the leaf or petal, about halfway around the dewdrop. If an additional painting is required, do it for the third firing; darken the colors applied in the second painting, once again being sure to leave the highlights completely free of color.

Black Raspberries

SEE COLOR PLATES 23 & 24, PAGES 30 & 31

Raspberries are an old, well-known fruit believed to have originated in Asia. Pliny (A.D. 24-79), in his writings on botany, mentions raspberries as wild fruits; in 1629, John Parkinson wrote of several varieties of raspberries, and their cultivation is presumed to have begun about this time.

Raspberries are classified as an aggregate fruit, which means that each small seed-bearing section (drupe) develops from one pistol of a single flower which contains several pistols. The relatively small leaves, which grow in clusters of three, are oval in shape and have saw-tooth edges.

These small fruits are fairly simple to paint and, while suitable subject matter by themselves, are often successfully combined into designs with flowers, such as wild roses and daisies.

FIRST PAINTING

Sketch the design of berries and leaves onto the china, or trace the design given here and transfer it to the piece with graphite paper.

Use a #6 shader brush to paint the leaves with yellow green, adding a touch of yellow brown to the main group of leaves near the berries.

Load a #10 shader brush with black green and paint the background areas to the left of the main group of leaves. Fill in the spaces between the leaves with the same color. Clean the brush and condition it in oil, then paint small areas

of mixing yellow in the upper left and lower right sections of the background. Apply loose strokes of pale blue to the remainder of the background.

Referring to the upper left section of the step-by-step color photos, block in the raspberries, as follows:

Corner-load a #6 shader brush with black and paint a row of small "C" strokes along the lower right side of each berry (see Fig. 1). Paint another row of similar strokes inside of and overlapping those in the first row (see Fig. 2), so that about half of each berry is covered with color. Using a mixture of black and blue (mixed on the brush), paint a row of "C" strokes around the remaining unpainted edge of each berry (see Fig. 3). Then fill in the rest of each berry with the same color mixture (see Fig. 4). For the small unripe berry at the left side of the design, corner-load the brush with pompadour, and paint the entire area with overlapping "C" strokes.

At this point, the painting should resemble the upper left section of the color photo.

Dip a #2 shader brush in turpentine, then press it against the paint cloth, to re-move as much of the turpentine as possible. With the brush conditioned in this manner as often as necessary, wipe out the little individual sections from the left (highlighted) side of each berry (see Fig. 5). Do not attempt to wipe these small sections perfectly free of color, but allow the pale color tone which results from this procedure to remain.

Corner-load the #6 shader brush with brown green and a little brown and paint the stem.

Fire the china to cone 017, then lightly sand it and wipe it with an alcohol-dampened cloth.

SECOND PAINTING

Deepen the background colors, paying particular attention to the angles formed by the joining of the design elements.

Model the leaves, using yellow brown, brown, and brown green for the upper group, and brown green and olive green for the lower group. Form the saw-tooth edges on the leaves by pulling the leaf colors out into the background.

Paint the separate sepals on the berries and the small stems with brown green.

Wash over the shadow side of each large berry with a rich coat of black, and over the shadow side of the unripe berry with violet-of-iron. Use a small brush to paint sharp black accents between the small, individual sections on the highlight sides of the berries (see Fig. 6), but avoid outlining the segments or the entire berry will lose the desired round look.

Darken the color on the shadow side of the main branch, using brown green and brown.

Fire the piece to cone 017.

If necessary, deepen any areas which may be weak in color, but avoid covering any part of the design with another complete coat of color.

Painting Birds

PART 1

SEE COLOR PLATES 25 & 26, PAGES 32 & 33

Scientists estimate that birds first appeared on the earth more than 140 million years ago, when some tree-climbing creature's scales began to evolve into feathers, to aid it in remaining aloft during leaps from branch to branch and tree to tree. The oldest fossil feather imprint dates from this time, and belonged to a creature called an Archaeopteryx, or ancient wing. While this unique creature was nothing like birds as we know them — it had teeth, a long, bony tail, and claws on its wings — it was definitely a bird, according to the accepted definition; a bird is described as an animal with feathers.

How many different kinds of birds evolved? We have no way of knowing. We do know, however, that at this time there are eight or nine thousand species of birds throughout the world. Of this vast number, well over seven hundred are found in North America. In order to more easily differentiate between the many species of birds, biologists have assigned to them twenty-eight major headings, or "orders." Each order contains many species and sub-species with the largest being the order "Passeriformes," comprised of the perching birds; this order is the highest developed and embraces more than half of all species. Most

BLACK-CAPPED CHICKADEE

THE LINE BETWEEN THE SIDES OF THE CHIN AND THE THROAT IS CALLED A WHISKER.

THE LOWER BACK IS CALLED THE RUMP AND TERMINATES IN FEATHERS CALLED THE UPPER TAIL COVERTS.

SPACE BETWEEN EYE AND BEAK IS CALLED THE LORE

CROWN
FOREHEAD
UPPER MANDIBLE
LOWER MANDIBLE
CHIN
THROAT
SHOULDER
BREAST
SIDE
BELLY
EYE RING
NAPE
EAR PATCH
BACK
WING BARS
SECONDARIES
PRIMARIES
TAIL
FLANK
TARSUS
OUTER TAIL FEATHERS
DIGIT
CLAW

members of the order Passeriformes are small birds, generally recognized as "song birds."

Artists have long been attracted by birds as subject matter, as attested by bird figures painted on the walls of the Lascaux cave in France, and in ancient hieroglyphs in Egypt. Literature is also filled with references to birds – the dove, raven, sparrow and others are mentioned in the Bible.

Contemporary interest in bird life has increased by leaps and bounds in recent years, which is easy to understand since birds are surely one of the most attractive and fascinating features of animate nature.

China painters, too, seem to be drawn more and more to the use of birds as subject matter, and the medium does lend itself extremely well to their portrayal. For those painters who have not as yet attempted to depict on china these intriguing bits of nature, it is hoped that this and subsequent chapters will serve as an impetus to a most rewarding endeavor.

Most china painters will probably not wish to spend too much time delving into ornithology – the study of birds. It is recommend, however, that one or two bird books be obtained, for reference; several very good but inexpensive books are readily available. The use of reference material is suggested, so that, whatever birds are being portrayed, they may be depicted with some accuracy. Most china painters who have had some experience can "whip up" a rose or other flower without referring to a study, but the same thing would hardly be true when painting birds. Each type of bird has physical characteristics uniquely its own, and may differ greatly in members of the same family, making good reference material a must for reasonably accurate portrayal.

Another definite help is to have some knowledge of the terminology used in describing a bird's various parts, so that written directions may be more easily followed. The accompanying drawing lists the major parts of the body surface of a bird (based on a chickadee), and will be referred to in later chapters.

It is also recommended that the painter select, for the first

few attempts, birds which are rather plain in color with little or no markings, such as the chickadees pictured in the color photo. The plainer birds are, naturally, easier to paint, and those with more variety in color and markings may be painted more freely after such practice.

One other suggestion is that, unless the painter is an accurate draftsman, all sketching be done on paper and the refined drawing transferred to the china with graphite paper. If the sketching is done directly on the china, constant erasures and changes eventually leave a smeary, messy, unpleasant surface on which to paint, whereas a tracing assures a clean, unsmudged painting surface.

When using a sheet of graphite paper for the first time, firmly wipe the graphite side with a facial tissue or a paper towel, to remove the excess graphite, so the traced lines will be very fine; a sheet of graphite paper treated in this manner actually seems to improve with use. A fine stencil stylus or a fine ballpoint pen, used for tracing the design, will also eliminate the possibility of having too heavy traced lines.

The directions which follow are for painting chickadees — ingratiating acrobats of the bird world. Chickadees are small birds measuring about 4-1/2" (those in the color photo are about life size), and are seen throughout much of the United States, as well as in parts of Canada. Constantly on the move, these tiny bundles of energy use their sharp, pointed bills to probe every crease and crevice of tree trunks and branches, to search out various forms of insects and larva which make up their diet. Often seen near feeders (especially if suet is offered), chickadees are easy to tame and will readily take food from the hand. The male and female are similar, and the young are miniature — if somewhat ragged — copies of the parents.

FIRST PAINTING

Trace all or part of the design given here onto a piece of thin paper, then transfer it to the china with graphite paper.

Corner-load a #6 or #8 square shader brush with black and, starting just above the bill, paint the forehead, crown and nape. Leave a thin un-painted line around the eye and a highlight at the base of the crown. Paint the bib with black, then use the corner of the same brush load to paint the bill.

Paint the entire eye with a light coat of red brown; then use a sharpened brush handle to push out a small highlight. Birds' eyes are not merely black spots, as we often see them painted; the irises are usually brown, although some birds — mockingbirds, some thrashers and others — have yellow irises and a few have eyes which are almost white, red and other colors.

Corner-load a shader brush with a neutral grey color, and shade the ear covets. Shade the back of the head with the same color, to add dimension with a look of roundness.

Paint the back and rump with yellow brown and brown (mixed on the brush), applying the color more heavily along the outer edge and above the wing.

Use a small, shader brush corner loaded with black, to paint separately each feather in each section of the wing. Paint the tail in the same manner.

Use yellow brown for the sides and flanks, and lightly shade the breast and belly with gray.

Paint the legs and feet black, leaving a highlight along the entire length of each leg, to make it appear tubular.

Wash over the leaves with yellow green (the shrub on which the birds are sitting is a cotoneaster divaricatus — a member of the rose family).

Paint the fruit with persian red, being sure to leave a large highlight on each one (see Chapter 12 for specific directions for portraying round forms).

Use brown and black green for the branches.

While the painting in the color photo has no painted background, background can be added at this time, if desired. Color suggestions for the background would be tints of blue (to represent the sky) and muted tones of green (for the effect of additional out-of-focus foliage).

Fire the piece to cone 017, then lightly sand it and wipe it with an alcohol-dampened cloth.

The piece at this stage should resemble the upper section of the step-by-step color photo.

SECOND PAINTING

When painting birds, most modeling and shading is done on the second painting. Since the eyes seem to be what brings the bird to life, they are completed first; paint them, wipe them off and re-paint them, as often as is necessary, to be sure they are lifelike, as follows:

Using a fine, pointed brush and black, paint a large pupil in each eye, carefully avoiding the highlight. Then paint a fine line of black completely around the eye. Fill in the area between the pupil and the outline on the top 1/3 of the eye, leaving a crescent shape of the original brown color showing in the lower portion; if necessary, clean out the crescent area with a clean brush.

Paint the various sections of the bird in the same order as the first painting, with the same colors.

Deepen the colors on the cap, bib and beak, being sure to leave highlights, to avoid a flat look to these parts. Wipe out the highlight on the upper mandible of the bill.

Use short, choppy strokes of gray to model the white parts of the head, pulling some of this color directly under the eye, to give a rounded look to the ear coverts.

Use a black and brown mixture on the back and rump, being sure to leave a highlight in the section directly above the wing.

Build up the color on the wing and tail feathers, shading deeply where one feather appears to be overlapped by another.

Paint the sides and flanks with a mixture of yellow brown and a touch of rich brown, using short, over-lapping strokes, to give a soft, fluffy look to these areas. Use grey to model the remainder of the body.

Corner-load a small shader brush with black, and use it to paint down the outer edges of the legs. Deepen the color between the toes. Use a pointed brush to indicate the scales on the legs and feet.

Shade the leaves with brown green and black green, adding a touch of persian to these colors in the shadow areas.

Deepen the color on the

lower side of each berry. Use a liner brush and black green to paint the bud ends.

Fire the piece to cone 017.

THIRD PAINTING

Deepen the color in any areas which seem weak, but do not completely cover any area.

Fire the piece again to cone 017.

It is difficult to say just how many paintings any piece will need before it can be considered to be complete. Everyone has his own method of applying color; some prefer many light coats, while others manage with 2 or 3 fairly heavy paintings. The thing the painter must decide for himself is when a painting is finished; it is as important to know when to stop as it is to know when to add more color — experience and personal preference are the only things that will actually solve this problem.

Painting Birds

PART 2

SEE COLOR PLATES 27 & 28, PAGES 34 & 35

Throughout the southeastern section of the country, the shrill call of "Pet-er! Pet-er! Pet-er!" announces the presence of tufted titmice. These somewhat drab little birds are close relatives of the chickadee and behave in the same, acrobatic manner while searching for insects among the leaves, branches and twigs of trees. Tufted titmice are slightly larger than chickadees (from 5-1/2" to 6" in length), and are common in wooded areas. Often associating with chickadees, warblers and kinglets, tufted titmice will frequent feeding stations in or near wooded locations, and (with patience) can be coaxed into taking food from the hand. Even though their main diet is made up of insects, titmice have a weakness for sunflower seeds and thin-shelled nuts, which they open by holding them in their feet and breaking them open with blows of their stout bills.

In coloration, tufted titmice have grey upper parts, white under parts and reddish flanks; the sexes are similar.

Titmice make excellent subjects for china painters who are new to bird painting, since they, like the chickadees in PART 1 of this chapter, have well defined areas of color and do not have the abundance of markings common in some birds. The painting in the color photo shows a pair of titmice in the branches of a weeping birch tree, in the spring of the year.

FIRST PAINTING

Place a piece of thin paper over the full-size pattern given

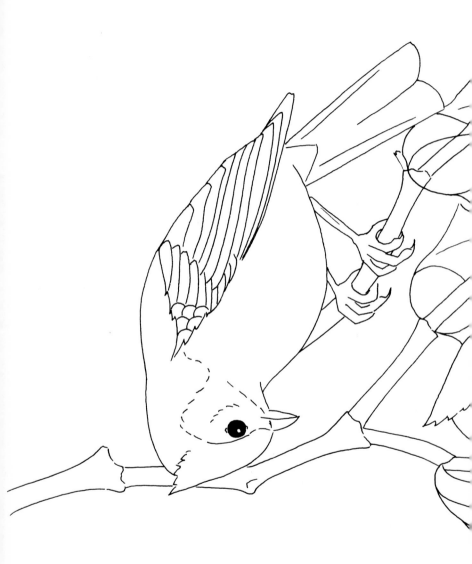

here, and trace all of the outlines and details. Transfer the pattern to the china, with graphite paper.

Beginning with the bird at the top of the design (if the lower bird were to be painted first, it could be smeared while the top one is being painted), paint the eye with red brown. Use a stenographer's eraser pencil or a sharpened brush handle to wipe out a clean highlight. Paint a line of black along the top edge of the upper mandible, and paint the lower mandible solidly with the same color. Firmly press the brush against the paint cloth, then use it to blend the line of black on the upper mandible into the unpainted area of the bill.

Corner-load a shader brush (#4 or #6) with black and paint the forehead. Pick up some Copenhagen blue on the same brush and paint the crown and crest; blend this color into the black on the forehead. Use the same blue black mixture for the nape, adding more black at the edges of the crest, for a shadow effect. Mix together on the brush some Copenhagen grey, black and a little brown, and paint the back.

Clean the brush and condi-

tion it in oil, then corner-load it with Copenhagen grey or some other light, neutral grey. Paint the cheek patch with this color, using short, choppy strokes to achieve a fluffy appearance.

Load a small, shader brush with grey and pick up a little black on one corner of it. Paint the wing feathers with these colors, keeping the black corner of the brush toward the bird's back, so that the feathers will appear to overlap each other in a natural manner. Paint the tail feathers with the same colors, keeping the black toward the outer edges.

Lightly shade the breast and belly with pale grey, being sure to leave a large highlight, so that these areas won't appear to be flat. Paint the under tail coverts with the same color. Paint the sides and flanks with streaks of dark yellow brown, applying the color more heavily near the wing and fading it off into the belly.

Corner-load a small shader brush with black and paint the legs and feet. If necessary, clean the brush and condition it in oil and wipe out a highlight down the length of each leg, to assure a rounded look.

Wash over the leaves with yellow green, adding a touch of warm brown green to separate one leaf from another where they overlap. Paint the catkins with short strokes of yellow brown, adding a little rich brown near the edges. Block in the branches with a mixture of brown and black.

While the finished painting pictured here does not have color in the background, background coloring may be added at this time, if desired. Suggested colors for the background are pale blue (for the atmosphere), black green (for distant foliage) and a little yellow (for sunlight).

Fire the china to cone 017, then lightly sand it and wipe it with an alcohol-dampened cloth. The painting should then resemble the area marked "FIRST PAINTING" in the step-by-step color photo.

SECOND PAINTING

Paint the birds' eyes, as follows:

Using a fine-pointed brush, paint a black pupil in the center of the eye, carefully avoiding the highlight. Paint a fine line of black completely around the eye, then fill in the area between the pupil and the outline at the top of the eye; when painted in this manner, a small, crescent shape of the original red brown color should be visible in the lower portion of the eye.

Deepen the color on the bill, being careful to retain the highlight on the upper mandible. Paint a tiny triangle of black at the base of the upper mandible, for the nostril.

Apply black to the forehead just above the bill, gently fading off the color into the crest. Using a mixture of Copenhagen blue and black on the corner of a small shader brush, paint a series of short strokes on the crest, to indicate rows of feathers.

Model the nape with Copenhagen blue and black, then add a speck of brown to the mixture and paint the back.

Darken the wing feathers with the same colors used for the first painting, being sure to accent the overlapping of the separate feathers by using the darkest tone wherever one feather goes under another. Using grey and a touch of black, deepen the color on the tail, accenting the overlapping of the feathers in the center. Paint a fine line of the black and grey mixture down each side of the tail, to indicate the quills of these feathers.

Add a little more color to the breast and belly areas, once again using short strokes to indicate feather texture; be sure to retain highlights, to increase the rounded, 3-dimensional look. Use dark yellow brown and a bit of rich brown for the sides and flanks. Allow these areas to dry for a few minutes, then cut through them with a clean, oil-conditioned brush, to heighten the look of fluffy feathers.

Use a fine-pointed brush to add the details to the legs and feet. With the same brush, lightly stipple an extremely fine line of black around each eye, about the width of a pencil line from the edges of the eyes; do not make this line too dark or too solid (see the color photo).

Shade the leaves with olive green and brown green, adding a little shading green for the deepest shadows. Use the corner of a clean, oil-conditioned brush to wipe out veins from several of the leaves.

Go over the catkins with tiny strokes of dark yellow brown, rich brown and a little brown green. Then clean the brush and use it to push out small highlights down the length of each catkin. Paint the leaf stems with olive green and brown green, and the catkin stems with yellow brown and rich brown.

Use a brown black mixture (more brown than black) to shade the branches, being sure to retain the rounded look by leaving good highlights.

Fire the piece to cone 017, then lightly sand it and wipe it with an alcohol-dampened cloth.

THIRD PAINTING

Strengthen any areas which are weak in color tone, but avoid covering any area completely. It is possible that the feather separations will need to be accented, and the shadow color where one group of feathers overlaps another may need deepening.

Fire the piece to cone 017.

Painting Birds

PART 3

SEE COLOR PLATES 29 & 30, PAGES 36 & 37

Outside of the breeding season, the golden-crowned kinglet is a gregarious bird, often seen enjoying the company of chickadees, nuthatches and brown creepers, along with an occasional woodpecker. Being about 3-1/2" to 4" in length, golden-crowned kinglets are, with the exception of some hummingbirds, the smallest birds of North America. Easily identified by their black-and-white-bordered crown patches, the sexes are similar, differing only in the color of the crown patches themselves — yellow with a red orange center in the male, and yellow in the female.

Golden-crowns always nest in some type of conifer (usu-ally spruce), and spend much of their time high in the branches searching out insects, larvae and eggs, which comprise their diet. During the summer months, they do feed lower down in the trees, where they can be identified (from other small birds) by the kinglet habit of repeatedly flicking their wings.

The china painter should encounter no problems in painting these little birds, since their bodies are quite plain and the eyepatches and crowns are distinct.

FIRST PAINTING

Make a careful tracing of the full-size pattern given here, then transfer the design to the

197

china with graphite paper. As suggested in an earlier part of this chapter, paint from the top of the design toward the bottom, to avoid smearing painted areas as the work progresses.

Use a small shader brush to paint the eye with red brown; then, with a sharpened eraser pencil or a brush handle, wipe out a sharp highlight.

Paint the bill and the crown patch black, leaving a highlight on the upper mandible of the bill. Paint a line of mixing yellow just above the crown patch on the male bird, and fill the remaining area of the crown with persian red; paint the entire crown of the female with mixing yellow. Use black for the eye patches, carefully leaving a fine line unpainted around each eye, to represent the eyelid (the eyelid should not be confused with an eyering — a definite ring of color around the eye, seen on some other birds). Lightly paint each of the ear coverts with pale brown, then stroke in a black whisker immediately below it.

Use a mixture of brown, black and grey (mixed on the brush) for the shoulder and back, adding a touch of green for the rump of the female.

Load a small, shader brush with brown and pick up a touch of black on the corner of the same brush. With the brush loaded in this manner, paint each wing feather separately, holding the brush so that the black-tipped corner is toward the bird's back. Allow the color on the wing feathers to dry for a few minutes, then use a clean, oil-conditioned brush to wipe out the wing bars and lines from the center of the leading edges of the primary feathers. Wash a little mixing yellow over the wiped-out areas on the primary feathers.

Paint the underside of the male bird's tail with grey and a little brown. Paint the female's tail with a mixture of brown and black. Wipe out the edges of the outer tail feathers, then wash over the wiped-out areas with mixing yellow.

Add a tiny bit of brown to some grey, and paint the entire front and underside of each bird's body, being sure to leave good highlights for a rounded appearance. Use a mixture of grey and black for the feet and legs.

Paint the branches with a mixture of brown, black and

black green. To paint the leaves, load a #4 round shader brush with yellow green and, starting with the tip of the brush at the stem end, draw the brush out a short distance from the trunk and press down. Wipe the color from those leaves which are to appear to be on top of others.

Fire the china to cone 017. Lightly sand the piece, then wipe it with an alcohol–dampened cloth.

SECOND PAINTING

In order to capture a lifelike feeling in the birds, paint their eyes first, as follows: Load a fine, pointed brush with black and paint a large pupil in the center of the eye, carefully avoiding the highlight. Then paint a fine line of black around the outer edge of the eye. Fill in the area between the pupil and the outline on the upper 1/3 of the eye, leaving a crescent shape of the original brown color visible in the lower portion; if necessary, clean out the crescent shape with a clean brush.

Paint the various sections of the birds in the same order as the first painting, with the same colors, striving to attain a 3-dimensional effect by paying careful attention to highlights and shadows.

Deepen the colors of the crown patches, using short, choppy brushstrokes, to depict the texture of feathers. Lightly shade the white patches above the eyes, with pale grey. Darken the color on the bills, being sure to retain the highlights on the upper mandibles.

Accent the separate wing feathers, by pulling a fairly deep tone of brown and black along the under edge of each one. Add some choppy strokes of grey brown to the backs of both birds and to the female's rump. Deepen the color on the tails, accenting the individual feathers. Use a mixture of grey, brown and a little black along the flanks at the edges of the wings.

Darken some grey with a little black, and, using a fine, pointed brush, paint tiny lines to indicate the scales on the legs and feet.

Model the leaves with brown green and shading green. Use the shading green on those leaves which appear to be under others, and on those which are to appear to recede into the background. Paint a fine center vein in each leaf.

Darken the color on the branches, being sure to retain a good highlight, so that the impression of roundness remains.

Fire the china to cone 017, then lightly sand it and wipe it with an alcohol-dampened cloth.

THIRD PAINTING

Touch up any areas which are weak in color, and add sharp accents wherever necessary. As directed in previous chapters, do not completely cover any area with color on the third painting – or the 3-dimensional effect may be lost. Use this (or whichever painting is to be last) to add only fine details and accents.

Painting Birds

PART 4

SEE COLOR PLATES 31 & 32, PAGES 38 & 39

Beginning with simple-to-paint birds, in Part 1 of this chapter, and progressing to those which present more of a challenge (due to configuration and markings), this chapter deals with a pair of birds which will require somewhat more care in painting. Complexity of pose or pattern need not, however, deter the beginning china painter from attempting these or other "difficult" subjects, if the painting is carried out one step at a time and the necessary depth of colors is developed gradually. It is all too common to be intimidated by a design which appears to be beyond one's capabilities, but that same design taken part-by-part often

proves to be no more difficult than some very basic pattern. The painter should train himself to mentally break down designs into their component parts and tackle each one separately.

The birds pictured in the color photo are a pair of Blackburnian warblers, common in spruce-fir forests of south-eastern Canada and much of the eastern portion of the United States; in the Appalachian region, they frequent stands of oak trees. These small (4-1/2" to 5-1/2" long) birds were named for a Mrs. Blackburn, an English-woman of the late 1700's, who was interested in birds. This is one instance when a name given to birds is quite fitting, since they are partly black and the male's orange breast does indeed seem to "burn" with brightness.

Blackburnian warblers spend much of their time high in the tops of trees, so it often takes a keen and knowledge-able person to locate and identify them in their natural surroundings.

FIRST PAINTING

Make an exact tracing of the full-size pattern given here, then transfer it to the china with graphite paper. If desired, go over the traced lines with india ink, as described in Chapter 13. Work from the top of the design (that is, paint the top bird first) toward the bottom, to avoid smearing previously painted areas as the work progresses.

Use a small (#4) square shader brush to paint the heads, backs, wings and tails of the birds, and a larger brush for the breast and belly areas.

Paint the entire eye with red brown, then wipe out a sharp highlight, using a sharpened eraser pencil or a brush handle.

Corner-load the small shader brush with black and lightly paint the beak, being

sure to indicate the separation between the mandibles. Clean the brush and use it to wipe a large highlight from the upper mandible.

Lay in the patch on top of the head, the stripe above the eye, the small patch below the eye and the stripes on the back, all with golden orange.

NOTE: Golden orange and the other orange color to be used later are fugitive colors — they should not be mixed with ANY yellow paint and should be applied more heavily than is usual for other colors. Any yellow mixed with the orange colors will cause them to fade completely away during the firing — as will a too-thin application.

Load the brush with black, and, starting just above the bill, paint the stripe along the crown and nape and down the back. Use the corner of the brush to gently pull the black color on the head stripe into the orange areas, for a feathery look. Apply black to the patch immediately in front of the eye and to the patch in back of the eye extending the color down to the shoulders. Gently wipe a highlight from the center of the back, and from the feathers along the edge of the shoulder.

Referring to the color photo and starting at the shoulder, paint each black wing feather with a corner-loaded brush, keeping the darkest color tone toward the bird's back, so that the feathers will appear to overlap one another in a natural manner; carefully avoid the areas which are to remain white. Paint the tail feathers in the same manner. Shade the white wing feathers with gray.

Using a #8 or #10 shader brush, paint the throat and breast with golden orange. Paint the flanks and belly with a gray made of brown, gray and a touch of black green, mixed together on the brush.

Apply a light coat of black to the leg and foot. Clean the brush and condition it in oil, then wipe out a highlight down the center of the leg and along the top of each toe.

Paint the female bird's bill and eye as described above, being sure to wipe out a high-light in the eye.

Use brown for the forehead, nape and cheek patch, leaving a good highlight on the lower part of the cheek. Paint the wing feathers with brown and black, mixed together on the brush. Pick up a little more black on the same brush and paint the outer tail feathers.

Apply golden orange to the eye stripe, the throat and the breast patch. Wipe out a stripe on the throat, from the bill to the breast. Use a mixture of brown and gray to lightly paint the remainder of the body, the lower tail coverts and the center tail feathers. Pick up a little brown on the corner of the same brush and, with short, choppy strokes, indicate the separation between the body and the tail coverts and between the tail coverts and the tail. Paint the legs and feet with black, as directed for the male bird.

Paint the branches with a brush corner-loaded with brown and black. With the color toward the outer edge on one side of the branch, paint its full length, then turn the piece and paint the other side; keeping the darkest color toward the outer edges will make the branch appear rounded.

Use the small brush to apply dark pink to the buds; then paint the calyxes with pale green, pulling the color over the edges of the buds.

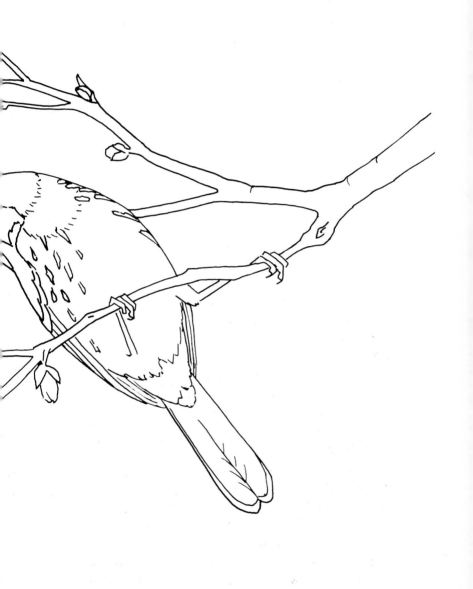

Fire the piece to cone 017; then lightly sand it, and wipe the surface with an alcohol dampened cloth.

The lower half of the step-by-step color illustration shows the piece as it should appear after the first firing.

SECOND PAINTING

Carefully position the tracing of the design on the china, lining up the traced outlines with the painting. Hold the tracing in place with one hand and slip a piece of graphite paper under it with the other. Now, trace just the spots on the birds' bodies. Remove the pattern and graphite paper, and go over the traced outlines with india ink.

Load a fine, pointed brush with black and paint a large pupil in the male bird's eye, carefully avoiding the highlight. Then paint a fine line of black around the outer edge of the eye. Fill in the area between the pupil and the outline on the upper 1/3 of the eye, leaving a crescent shape of the original red brown color visible in the lower portion; if necessary, clean out the crescent shape with a clean brush.

Apply color to the various sections of the bird in the same order as directed for the first painting, using the same colors — except on the golden orange areas. Shade the golden orange areas with dark orange, applying this color more heavily along the edge of the body and near the shoulder. Be sure to leave a large highlight of the original color, to give the body a rounded, 3-dimensional look.

Corner-load the small shader brush with black and paint the spots on the body along the wing outline. Hold the china so that the brush-strokes for the spots are pulled toward the bird's head, and hold the brush so the bristles are at about a 45° angle in relation to an imaginary line down the center of the spot. Painted in this manner, the markings should taper to a point at their upper ends.

Use the small, pointed brush and black paint to indicate the scales on the leg and foot.

Darken the colors on the female in the same manner, using the same colors used in the first painting. After shading the throat and breast patch, add a little dark orange to the edges of these areas; do not apply a complete coat of the dark orange, as the female should not be as bright as the male.

Deepen the color on the branch with a mixture of brown, black and black green, once again retaining the highlight along the full length of each section. Shade the buds with dark pink, indicating separations between petals with the same color. Shade the calyxes with brown green. Fire the piece to cone 017, then sand and wipe it as done before.

In all probability the deep orange color will have faded somewhat due to the temperature required to mature the other colors. This is common when using cadmium-based (orange) paints, and can be remedied as directed below:

THIRD PAINTING

Apply more color to any areas which seem weak, and add sharp accents where necessary. Touch up the dark orange areas of the male's breast once again, applying a heavier coat than is usual.

To "hold" this orange color, fire the piece to cone 017, as follows: The enemies of cadmium-based colors are excessive heat and lack of oxygen, so for the final firing vent the kiln by propping open the lid about 4" until the interior glows dull red. Also, reduce the firing time by advancing the kiln switches every 30 to 45 minutes, instead of the usual recommended 1 to 1-1/2 hours. When the firing is complete (the cone bends or the automatic shut off device operates), use a claw hammer, heavy coat hanger, etc. to open the kiln lid about 1" for a few moments, to prevent further heat build-up. Then close the lid and allow the kiln to cool in the usual manner.

If the orange colors fade again (they are the "Peck's Bad Boy" of china paints), do not be discouraged or alarmed. Simply reapply only the orange color and fire to a lower temperature – cone 018 or 019. Record the results of firing your particular orange colors, to follow when these colors are used in future projects.

Painting Birds

PART 5

SEE COLOR PLATES 33 & 34, PAGES 40 & 41

Song sparrows like those pictured in the color photo are one of this country's most abundant birds, and should be familiar to almost everyone. These birds do, however, vary from one area to another, as each of the thirty-one recognized subspecies has adapted to its own particular habitat. Adaptability is a strong characteristic of many sparrows, but is especially true of song sparrows, which are "right at home" in city and country situations. Song sparrows are to be found wherever there is fresh water and enough dense cover for their feeding and nesting needs.

These birds almost always nest at or near ground level, and are busy most of the summer raising anywhere from two to four broods of young.

Song sparrows can readily be identified by their heavily marked backs and sides; the side markings converge at a central breast spot, which birders use as a field mark. Another identifying feature of song sparrows is their habit of repeatedly pumping their tails up and down. They may also be recognized by their call and song; the call is a metallic *chink* or *chirp,* and the song has been likened in cadence to the phrase, "hip, hip, hurray boys, spring is here." This melodious song can be heard throughout the spring and summer, and, at times, in the dead of winter.

Unlike the plainer birds in foregoing sections of this chapter, which have rather large areas of smooth color, it is necessary to paint individual feathers on heavily marked birds as depicted here.

FIRST PAINTING

Make a careful tracing of the pattern given here. Use graphite paper to transfer the design to the china, omitting the feather outlines on the backs (these feathers will be painted later).

Beginning with the top bird, paint the eye with red brown, then use an eraser pencil or a sharpened brush handle to knock out a highlight.

Using a small shader brush and dark brown, lightly lay in the stripes on the forehead and nape. Paint the eye patch with the same color, leaving a fine, unpainted line completely around the eye. Use the same dark brown for the whisker and the edge of the cheek, pulling a series of small comma strokes toward the beak, to obtain a feathered look in these areas. Wash over the cheek with pale brown, leaving a large highlight in the center.

Mix together on the brush some grey and dark brown, and apply a light coat of the mixture to the bird's back. Corner-load the brush with dark brown and, with the color-loaded corner toward the bird's back, paint each wing feather separately. Paint the edge of the tail with the same color and the under side of it with grey. Indicate the feathers on the undertail coverts with short, overlapping strokes of brown.

Wash over the edges of the body and the breast with a mixture of yellow brown and grey, being sure to leave a large highlight in the center of the body, to impart a rounded look. Corner-load the brush with yellow brown and brown and paint the markings on the body, using a comma stroke for each one; use a series of overlapping comma strokes for the large spot in the center of the breast.

Paint the beak and the legs and feet with yellow brown. Lightly indicate the separation between the upper and lower mandible, with a fine line of brown.

Apply the same colors in the same order to the remaining bird, except the tail. On this bird, the upper surface of the tail is exposed, so paint the separate feathers with dark brown as directed for the wing feathers.

Lightly wash in the background, using pale blue for about the upper 2/3 of the area, black green for the lower 1/3, and one or 2 touches of mixing yellow, for warmth. Be sure to blend the background colors softly together.

Wash over the leaves with chartreuse or yellow green (this shrub is a blackthorn, and has rather glossy, slender leaves with serrated edges). Use a mixture of dark blue and black for the fruit, being sure to leave a large highlight in each one. Paint the branches with a mixture of dark brown and black green, and the thorns with a mixture of black and dark brown.

Fire the china to cone 017; then lightly sand it, and wipe it with an alcohol-dampened cloth.

SECOND PAINTING

Carefully reposition the pattern on the piece; then, while holding the pattern in place, slip a sheet of graphite paper under it. Trace over the feather outlines on the back of each bird. Remove the pattern and graphite paper.

Paint the birds' eyes first. Using a fine, pointed brush, paint a black pupil in the center of the eye, carefully avoiding the highlight; on the lower bird, the brow is partially obscuring the eye, so only about the lower half of the pupil will show. Paint a very fine line of black around the eye, then fill in the area between the pupil and the outline at the top of the eye; a small crescent of the original red brown color should show in the lower section of the eye.

Using a small shader brush corner-loaded with brown, shade the bill along the top of the upper mandible and the bottom of the lower one. Deepen the color on the lower mandible along the separation line. Pull in a tiny triangle of black at the base of the bill, for the nostril.

Darken the color on the head, using a mixture of dark brown and black for the brown stripes, and lightly shade the light stripes with grey. Pull some grey into the chin patch, adding a touch of

black directly under the bill. Deepen the color on the cheek under the eye and at the rear edge. Using tiny, short strokes of brown, gently add the feather pattern to the cheek.

Paint the individual back feathers with dark brown and black, allowing the original color to show along the edge of each one. Be sure that as each feather is painted the deepest color is pulled up under the ones which are directly above it. Deepen the colors on the wing feathers, in the same manner.

Paint the tail of the upper bird with grey and black, and the tail feathers of the lower one with dark brown and black.

Using a mixture of yellow brown, brown and touch of dark blue for greyness, shade the edges of the body, once again retaining a large highlight. Deepen the color on the body markings, then use a clean brush to feather off the wide end of each spot.

Paint the scales on the legs and feet, with fine lines of dark brown.

Use brown green and black green to model the leaves, lightly indicating vein lines on a few of them. Shade the fruit with dark blue and black (see Chapter 12, for directions on rendering round objects). Use brown green for the stems of the fruit.

Model the branches with dark brown, black green and black, and mixtures of these colors. Carefully retain a highlight along the length of each branch, for a rounded, 3-dimensional look.

Fire the piece to cone 017, then lightly sand and wipe it as before.

THIRD PAINTING

Use this, or whatever painting is to be the last, to deepen only areas which are weak in color and to add any necessary accents.

Fire the piece to cone 017.

Bird Miniatures

SEE COLOR PLATES 35 & 36, PAGES 42 & 43

Almost everyone has a problem selecting gifts for family and friends, and this seems to be especially difficult when trying to think of things for Christmas giving. The china painter does, however, have the advantage of being able to create gifts especially for the recipients, and the items can be personalized so they will know the gifts were made just for them. It is even possible to establish a tradition, by using the same style of china and design each year, incorporating the date in the design. The porcelain bisque bells pictured in the color photo were designed for this kind of Christmas gift.

Any type of piece could be used — small covered boxes, miniature plates or mugs, little plaques, etc. — and the style of the designs can be whatever the painter wishes, as long as there is continuity each year in the piece and the design.

Only one or two of the birds on the pictured bells were painted with any specific bird in mind, the others being painted in any colors which seemed to suit either the season or the foliage on which they are perched. The year was printed on the back of each bell, surrounded by holly sprays, mistletoe, pinecones and other seasonal motifs. In addition, some of the bells have bits of verse written on their sides. The bands around the tops and bottoms of the bells are painted in colors to complement the designs, or in gold or silver. Any personal message is printed on the inner rim.

The directions which follow are for the piece pictured separately in the color photo.

FIRST PAINTING

If the piece to be painted is porcelain bisque, thoroughly wet sand it with medium-fine wet or dry sandpaper, then wash and dry it.

Trace the pattern given here onto a piece of thin paper, and transfer it to the bell with graphite paper.

Use a detail brush to paint each bird's eye black, then wipe out a highlight with the point of a toothpick.

Load a #4 square shader brush with yellow brown and paint in the beaks. Pick up some brown on the same brush and paint the underside of the upper mandible of the bird which has the open beak. Apply a light coat of brown to each bird's "cap." Clean the brush and then corner-load it with grey, and paint the cheek patches. Using a mixture of grey, blue and a touch of green, paint the back of the foremost bird.

Clean the brush and corner-load it with brown. Paint the separate shoulder feathers, using a downward stroke with the color-bearing corner of the brush for each one. Use the edge of the brush to paint the long wing feathers, leaving a fine, unpainted line along the edge of each feather. Paint the tails with a mixture of grey, blue and a touch of black. Shade the edge of each bird's body with a mixture of grey and blue; then apply this same mixture under each wing, for a shadow.

Paint the feet with a liner brush and yellow brown. Lay in the branches with brown.

Sketch or trace the design on the back of the bell (the dotted lines on the pattern indicate shadow leaves and stems). Paint the leaves bright green and the berries persian red. Use a mixture of grey and green for the shadow leaves and stems. Load the pointed brush with bright green and carefully paint in the numbers.

Use the shader brush to apply a smooth coat of bright green to the bands around the top and bottom of the bell.

Fire the piece to cone 017, then lightly sand it and wipe it

with an alcohol-dampened cloth.

SECOND PAINTING

Shade the birds' caps just above the beaks with a mix-ture of brown and black, pulling some fine lines of color over the background to give the birds a fuzzy look. Shade

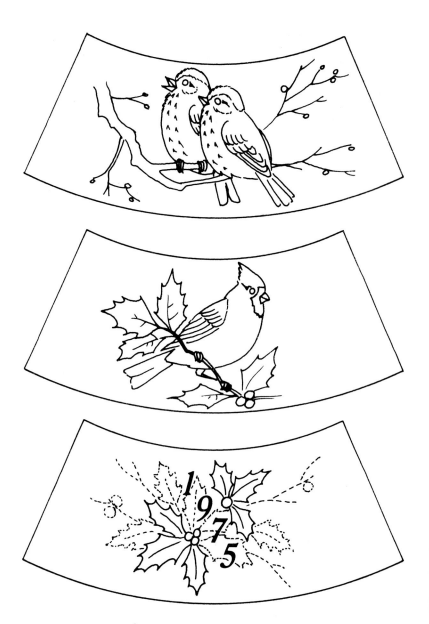

the upper and lower edge of
each beak, with a little brown.
Paint a tiny triangle of the
same brown color behind each
eye. Darken the colors on the
back and the wings, outlining

some feathers, if necessary, to
define them. Accent the separate tail feathers with a little
black, and pull a little brown
along the edge of the back
bird's tail.

Clean the brush and then pick up a little yellow brown on the left corner of it. Holding the bell upside down, paint tiny comma strokes on the breast of each bird, following the body contours. Use the pointed brush and black to accent the toes and to indicate the separation between the upper and lower mandibles of the foremost bird.

Shade the branches with dark brown and black. If this is to be the final painting, apply small dots of red enamel along the branches, for berries (always apply enamel only when the piece is to be fired for the final time).

Use black green to model the leaves around the date on the back of the bell and deepen the colors of the berries, if necessary.

Fire the piece to cone 017.

To paint the birds in the other patterns given here, follow the same general directions but vary the colors. Even though the birds may not be realistically painted, keep the colors rather subdued or greyed with accents of bright color, to impart a natural look. In addition, white enamel can be used on the last painting for "snow" along the tops of branches and leaves.

These same patterns can be altered for other holidays or gift-giving occasions, by adding flowers and foliage appropriate to the season, around the birds and the date.

Rufous-Sided Towhees

SEE COLOR PLATE 37, PAGE 44

Rufous-sided towhees are so distinctively marked and colored that there is little possibility of mistaking them for any other birds. Members of the finch family, towhees spend almost all of their time vigorously scratching through dead leaves and grasses in areas of dense brush and vegetation, in search of insects. The male bird may occasionally be seen in a tree, where he has established a "singing perch," but these tree-top visits are usually brief — and he makes frequent return flights to the ground cover, where he is more at home (and presumably more at ease). During the winter months, when their insect diet is not available, towhees will eat vegetable matter, and can be attracted to feeding stations if they are positioned near suitable cover.

The eastern subspecies of rufous-sided towhees have red eyes (these birds were once known as red-eyed towhees) and their name is derived from an attempt to imitate the call which sounds something like to-whee. The male has a black head and back, rufous (reddish) sides and white underparts: the female is similarly marked, but the head may vary from greenish-brown to almost black. In many species of birds, the female must take a back seat to the more resplendent males, but the female towhee is every bit

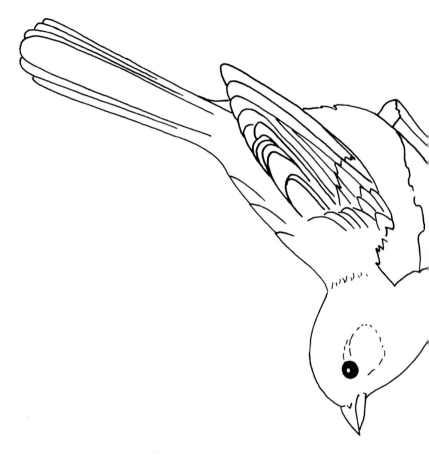

as handsome as her spouse. Both sexes of these birds make excellent subject matter for the china painter.

FIRST PAINTING

Make an accurate tracing of the full-size design given here, then transfer it to the china with graphite paper. If desired, go over the traced lines on the

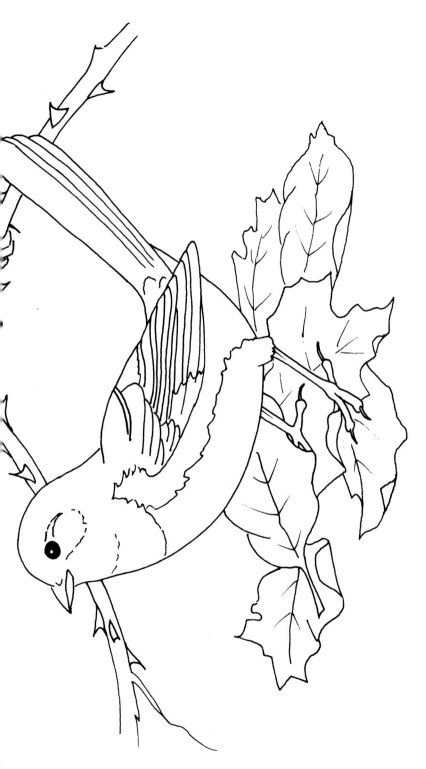

china with india ink, as described in Chapter 13. Paint from the top to the bottom of the design, to avoid smearing previously painted areas as work progresses.

Beginning with the male bird on the branch, paint the eye with persian red, then use an eraser pencil to wipe out a sharp highlight.

Corner-load a small shader brush and lightly paint the beak, being sure to leave a highlight along the upper mandible and indicate the separation between the upper and lower mandibles.

Using a larger (#8 or #10) shader brush and black, paint the head and back, leaving highlights above the eye, in the cheek and throat and on the center of the back. Corner-load the same brush with black and paint the individual wing feathers, carefully avoiding the white wing bar and the white edges of the large feathers. Paint the tail feathers in the same manner.

Apply a light coat of dark yellow brown to the shoulder, sides and belly, softly feathering the color into the lower body to avoid a sharp line along the edges of the yellow brown areas. Shade along the lower edge of the body with pale gray. Wash over the leg and foot with light yellow brown.

Paint the female bird in the same manner, substituting a mixture of brown and brown green for the black on the head, back, wings and tail.

Paint the leaves with broad strokes of color, to give them a crisp, dry look, using light and dark yellow browns, brown, brown green and violet of iron. Paint the branch and thorns with red brown and dark brown.

Apply a wash of pale blue to the sky area, leaving "windows," or open areas, for a light, airy look. Working from the leaves toward the sky, brush in some brown green and gray, for background foliage. Cut through this color with a clean, oil-conditioned brush, to simulate weeds.

Mix together some dark blue, black green and enough persian red to produce a "dirty" neutral gray color. Apply this mixture to the area directly under the leaves. Cut through this patch of color with the edge of a clean brush, criss-crossing the strokes, to give the appearance of earth and dead grass and weeds.

Fire the piece to cone 017, then lightly sand it and wipe it with an alcohol-dampened cloth.

SECOND PAINTING

Using a fine, pointed brush, paint a large pupil in the male bird's eye, carefully avoiding the highlight. Load the same brush with dark brown and paint a line around the edge of the iris. Clean and oil the brush, then soften the edge of the brown line, to give the eye a rounded appearance.

Corner-load the #4 shader brush with black and darken the color on the bill; be sure to retain a highlight on both mandibles, to preserve the 3-dimensional look.

Darken the color along the edges of the head, back, breast and cheek, striving to attain a rich black color on these areas without allowing the paint to pile up. Lightly brush a little pale blue in the highlight areas. Corner-load the same brush with black and use it to darken the color on the wing and tail feathers. Use a tiny bit of gray to indicate the feather separations on the white wing patch.

Deepen the shadow on the body under the wing, with a mixture of dark yellow brown and dark brown. Brush a little of this mixture along the edge of the body. Shade the belly with gray and a touch of black.

Use a liner brush and brown to paint the scales on the leg and foot.

Paint the female bird in the same fashion, shading the head, back, wings and tail with dark brown instead of black.

Deepen the color on the leaves, particularly in the areas where one leaf seems to be overlapped by another. Paint the shadows on the ground under the leaves, with a dark neutral gray mixture of persian red, dark blue and black green. Add shadows on the branch with dark brown.

Fire the piece to cone 017, then sand it and wipe it with an alcohol-dampened cloth.

THIRD PAINTING

Deepen the colors wherever necessary, but do not completely cover any area with color. Paint the claws on the female bird's feet, with a mixture of dark brown and black. Add sharp accents of color to the leaves, to heighten the dry, crisp look.

Fire the piece again to cone 017.

Evening Grosbeaks

SEE COLOR PLATE 38, PAGE 45

During the breeding season, evening grosbeaks make their home in northern forests of spruce, fir and related trees, but throughout the winter may be attracted to feeding stations where they will rapidly shell and devour quantities of sunflower seeds. Easily recognized by their large, powerful beaks, these gregarious birds often gather in large flocks in the fall and winter months — a thrilling and unforgetable sight for any bird lover.

The male bird's body is a beautiful golden yellow which contrasts sharply with his black and white wings, while the female's body is predominantly a soft grey — ample reason for a painter to select these birds as subject matter.

FIRST PAINTING

Make a tracing of the full-size pattern given here, then use graphite paper to transfer the design to the china.

Beginning with the male bird at the top of the pattern, paint the eye red brown. Use an eraser pencil or a sharpened brush handle to wipe a highlight from the eye.

Using a small (#4) square shader brush, paint the small area above the beak and the back of the head, black. Paint the cheek patch and neck with a mixture of black, dark brown and a touch of blue. With a mixture of tan, brown and enough black to grey the color, paint the upper breast and back; then paint the lower back and the area between the wings, with mixing yellow.

Pick up a little grey on the corner of a clean, conditioned brush, and paint the feather separations on the wing feathers which are to be white.

229

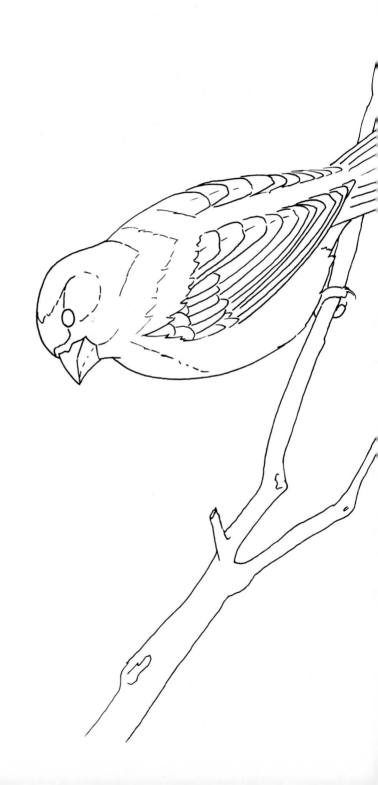

Corner-load the same brush with black, and paint the rest of the wing feathers and the tail. Use a clean, conditioned brush to apply mixing yellow to the forehead patch and to the breast and belly; gently feather the yellow into the color on the upper breast areas, so that there is no definite separation line between these colors.

Apply a light wash of tan to the beak, indicating the separation between the mandibles with a fine line of brown. Use the same tan color for the foot.

Paint the female bird's eye red brown, then wipe out a highlight as directed above.

Make a neutral grey tone by mixing together small amounts of dark blue, black green and persian red, adjusting the proportions so that no one color predominates. Use this mixture with a little black to paint the head, cheek patch, neck and upper back. Load the brush with the neutral grey tone, then pick up a little yellow brown, and apply this mixture to the area below the cheek patch and to the upper part of the wing. Paint the whisker (the area between the corner of the beak and the breast) with short strokes of black.

Indicate the separate feathers on the white portion of the wing, by lightly shading them with grey. Paint the remaining wing feathers and the tail black. Paint the breast, sides and belly with short strokes of the neutral grey mixture, being sure to leave a large highlight, to achieve a rounded look to the body.

Paint the upper mandible of the beak tan, and the lower mandible tan with a touch of black. Use tan for the legs and feet.

Use persian red for the caps of the fly amanita mushrooms, then wipe out scattered spots, to represent the scurf or scales which are characteristic of these particular mushrooms. Paint the stem and underside of the large mushroom with a dirty grey green (mix pale green, a touch of red and a little dark blue). Indicate the folds on the underside, with curved lines of brown green.

Wash a background of pale blue around the male bird, then work from the horizon line up to the blue with loose strokes of warm brown green. Using a mixture of tan, brown and a little green, paint horizontal strokes from the horizon line downward, to represent the earth. Corner load the brush with yellow green and pull up through the warm brown green background, to simulate blades of grass. Repeat this procedure with brown green and black green, then cut through the area with a clean brush, to provide variety of color and highlights in the grass. Pull some short strokes of green over the bases of the mushrooms, so that they will appear to be growing up through the grass.

Fire the china to cone 017; then lightly sand it, and wipe it with an alcohol-dampened cloth.

SECOND PAINTING

Paint the birds' eyes first. Using a fine, pointed brush, paint a black pupil in the center of the eye, carefully avoiding the highlight. Paint a fine line of black completely around the eye, then fill in the area between the pupil and the outline at the top of the eye, so that a small crescent of the original brown color shows in the lower section.

Corner-load a small shader brush with tan and a bit of brown, and shade the upper mandibles of the beaks. On the male bird, paint a small triangle of this color mixture on the bottom of the lower mandible, to give it a somewhat square look. Shade the entire lower mandible of the female bird's beak, since it is in shadow and not as clearly defined as the male's.

Using the same colors and color mixtures as for the first painting, deepen the colors on the heads, wings and tails. Shade the male's back, belly and sides with short, choppy strokes of dark yellow brown. Shade the female's body with the original neutral grey mixture. Indicate the scales on the legs and feet, with fine lines of dark brown.

Darken the branch with black, brown and black green, keeping most of the detail to the left, (heavy end), so that the right end will appear to recede into the background.

Shade the right sides of the mushroom caps with a mixture of persian red and brown, and add a tiny shadow under each white patch.

Mix together on the brush some tan, brown and a little black green, and paint a shadow on the ground under the female bird.

Fire the piece to cone 017; then lightly sand and wipe it, as before.

THIRD PAINTING

Use this painting to strengthen any areas which are weak in color and to add any necessary accents.

Fire the china again to cone 017.

**Pattern for the piece pictured
on the dust jacket**

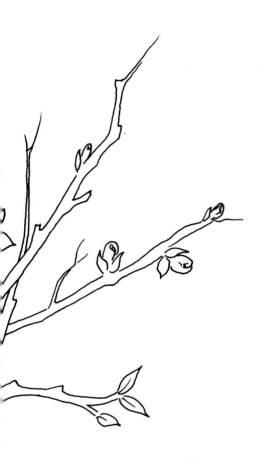

NOTES